# MOTHERS of MAGIC

## Summoning the Wisdom of Our Ancestors

PERDITA FINN

RUNNING PRESS
PHILADELPHIA

Running Press
Hachette Book Group
1290 Avenue of the Americas, New York, NY 10104
www.runningpress.com
@Running_Press

First Edition: May 2026

Published by Running Press, an imprint of Hachette Book Group, Inc.
The Running Press name and logo are trademarks of Hachette Book Group, Inc.



Cover illustration by Sarah Jarrett @sarahjarrettart
Print book cover and interior design by Susan Van Horn

Library of Congress Cataloging-in-Publication Data has been applied for.

ISBNs: 979-8-89414-065-0 (hardcover), 979-8-89414-066-7 (ebook)

Printed in the United States of America

LSC-C

Printing 1, 2026

for all my mothers

for Mum

for the ones to come

# CONTENTS

Reimagining the Mother ........ vii
The Bodies of Our Mothers ........ ix

**THE FIRST PART:**
OUR MOTHERS BEFORE PATRIARCHY ........ 1

Chapter One: Appetite Is Holy and Makes Us Wholly Us ........ 3
*A Message from the Old Ones* ........ 14

Chapter Two: The Fairy Godmothers ........ 19
*A Message from the Old Ones* ........ 29

Chapter Three: Make Love Not War ........ 31
*A Message from the Old Ones* ........ 45

*An Invitation: You Are Circled by Mothers* ........ 48

**THE SECOND PART:**
OUR MOTHERS WITHIN PATRIARCHY ........ 55

Chapter Four: The Stories We Tell, The Curses We Undo ........ 57
*A Message from the Oldest of Grandmothers* ........ 75

Chapter Five: Out of the Fires ........ 81
*A Message from an Old Mother* ........ 94

Chapter Six: Are You My Mother? ........ 101
*A Message from the Last Daughter at the End of the World* ........ 117

*An Invitation: Summoning the Hidden Power of Our Ancestral Mothers* ........ 120

**THE THIRD PART:**
OUR MOTHERS AFTER PATRIARCHY .......... *125*

Chapter Seven: A Foundation of Faith .......... *127*

*A Message from the Mothers of the Miraculous* .......... *136*

Chapter Eight: The Lies We Tell Ourselves .......... *139*

*A Message from the Mothers of Mystery* .......... *156*

Chapter Nine: Talking about Reality .......... *159*

*A Message from the Mothers of Magic* .......... *180*

*An Invitation: The Return of Our Mothers* .......... *183*

Dear Mothers to Come .......... 189
A Heart Spell .......... 193
Acknowledgments .......... 195
Notes .......... 201

# REIMAGINING THE MOTHER

When I was traveling in France on a second honeymoon with my husband Clark, I noticed that in many small churches the statue of the Virgin Mary was often flanked by two other figures. On one side of the Lady, Joan of Arc stood in full armor, brandishing her sword, while on the other was St. Anthony in his monk's robes, cradling the infant Jesus in his arms. Without consciously knowing it, the creators of these groupings had crafted shrines to the Holy Mother that implicitly acknowledged the many ways to show up in the world maternally. A woman could be a warrior who was a mother, and a mother could be a mystic who was a man. Neither Joan nor Anthony had biological children—but for centuries people around the world have turned to them in their hour of need for care and wisdom, guidance and love. They have turned to them as children seeking their mothers.

Mothers know that it takes many hands to raise a child. No wonder Kuan Yin, the Buddhist goddess of compassion, has a thousand arms. One of those hands is there to smooth a furrowed brow, while another brings us our armor before we head into battle. One hand guides our weaving, and another braids our hair. If we look to the folklore in any culture around the world, we find ourselves not ruled by a singular deity but instead circled by a pantheon of mothers. Reinforcing this is the fact that among many ancient peoples the number nine, the magical number of human pregnancy, was holy and sacred—there were nine muses in Greece, nine Icelandic goddesses, the blessed Ennead of the Egyptians, the nine expressions of the Hindu goddess Durga, and the nine original mothers of the Kogi people of Colombia.

These mothers, so many mothers, circle us with protection.

But we live in times where the mothers have been isolated, marginalized, vilified, and silenced. Being an actual mother has never been more narrowly defined. Only when I became a mother myself did I begin to understand how trapped I felt, how vast my own need for mothering really was—and how incapable a single person was of offering their children all that they demanded, all that they deserved. Out of my own longing and necessity for practical and spiritual mothering I began a decades-long investigation into what it really meant to be a mother.

What had it been like to be a mother before systems of domination defined our gender roles? What was it really like through the ages to be a mother within these oppressive religious and cultural institutions? How might changing our understanding of what it means to become a mother transform the world itself?

This book explores these questions over the course of nine chapters. Through an intimate examination of my relationship with my own mother, as well as historical and scientific realities, I offer, story by story, a gestational journey that I hope helps each of us transcend civilization's inherent misogyny and rebirth in our lives a renewed experience of vitality and love. The more I opened myself during the writing of this book to the wisdom of my ancestors, the more it began to flow through me. I offer to you the messages and stories of these old grandmothers as well.

Drawing on material from the workshops I have taught around the world, I also provide exercises and prompts to help readers access their own renewed relationship with the many maternal presences available to us here and on the other side. You will learn how to summon all kinds of mothers to answer prayers, alchemize relationships with your own mothers, and discover how connecting to our future mothers in incarnations to come transforms how we treat all beings each and every day.

Women will, of course, come to these insights more readily than men, but I hope that they will share this book with their fathers, their husbands, their brothers, and their sons. My wild dream is a world in which men envision themselves as mothers as surely as St. Anthony, in which women feel liberated from oppressive gender roles as boldly as St. Joan, in which each of us can join hands with the Blessed Mother, with the many mothers of all religions and traditions, to cradle and care for the very life force of this planet.

# THE BODIES OF OUR MOTHERS

Tell me about your mother's body—her hands and her feet, her belly and her breasts. Tell me about her skin and her hair and the color of her eyes. Tell me about her smell—her breath, her underarms, the scent of her when she leaned in close.

In the beginning I do not want to know your grievances with her. Do not tell me yet about how she failed you, disappointed you, infuriated you, frightened you. Do not tell me about your relationship with her, much as I know you want to confess and condemn, plead and implore. No, let us leave all that for now. Tell me about your mother's body.

If she were an animal—and she was, I tell you this, *she was*—how would you describe her?

Tell me about her fur and her funk, her fangs and her feathers. Did she fly? Did she burrow? Did she slither upon the ground or slink through the shadows of the forest at dusk or step into the meadow at noon with her head held high?

You have reached out your hand to lay it upon hers, and already I know you have begun to cry.

Her hands were dry; her hands were soft; her hands were chapped and cracked. Her nails were always polished; her nails were chipped; her nails were bitten down until they bled. Her fingers were thin and tapered or stubby and swollen. At the end of her life was her skin mottled with brown spots? Maybe you touched her hand after she died and felt it turn hard and cold beneath yours. Maybe she is still alive, but it is a long time since you imagined touching her. Maybe you look at your own hands and have begun to see hers.

Your mother's body was your first home in this life. Deep within the darkness of her womb you came into the knowing of who you might become, listening to her heartbeat, smelling her blood from within, feeling her muscles contract around your body. Her body creating your body.

My mother was a tiger, her languorous haunches moving stealthily through the jungle. My mother was a seal, her muscular body undulating in the waves. My mother was a crow, muttering irritated curses under her breath. My mother was a spider, a snake, a vole, a hawk. My mother was an animal.

Travel back in time and our ancestors will tell you that the goddesses, the most ancient mothers, had the wings of vultures, the heads of hippos, the paws of great cats, the tails of sea serpents, the bodies of buffaloes, reindeer, mammoths, and aurochs. Our Lady of the Beasts is the oldest name, after all, of the Madonna. Our Lady of the Beasts, a lion at her side, a snake in her hands, is herself a creature of this Earth.

Let us circle ourselves with these ancient mothers—with mothers who are bears, mothers who are owls, mothers who are spiders. The first magic that we will perform together is to turn our mothers back into the animals they have always been.

Let us give our mothers back their bodies: the appetites and desires of those bodies, the force and power of those bodies, the songs and howls and growls of those bodies.

I need to tell you about the body of my mother, and I need to hear about the body of your mothers. Together we must remember what was done to the bodies of our mothers—*all* of our mothers—because for a long time now their bodies, our bodies, the bodies of animals, the bodies of trees, the bodies of mountains, and the body of the Earth—all bodies—have been under attack.

THE FIRST PART

# OUR MOTHERS *before* PATRIARCHY

## Chapter One

# APPETITE IS HOLY AND MAKES US WHOLLY US

At the end of dinner, served on the fine china with the English silver, my mother would snap apart her chicken bones and suck out the marrow with her tongue. The candles glowed. The wax dripped. The bouquet of roses at the center of the table exuded a soft perfume. Our guests would look down at their white plates, moving an uneaten piece of oily lettuce back and forth with their polished forks, sated by my mother's cooking and embarrassed by her unembarrassed display of appetite.

My mother loved eating, drinking, fucking, and life itself, devouring it all with rapacious pleasure right down to the inside of the bones.

I grew up terrified she might devour me.

She made her own pâté, grinding up livers, kidneys, and other organ meats at the kitchen table. She cooked giant cow tongues on the top of the stove. She liked raw hamburger, which she'd sprinkle with a little salt and hand to me, licking her wet tongue across her lips, waiting for me to see just how delicious bloody flesh could be.

Once a month she drove to Boston to collect used-up lab rats to feed to our boa constrictor. She would watch blithely as the rats' plump white bodies disappeared into his maw. She wore the boa constrictor around her neck, delighted by the feel of his smooth, muscled body against her skin. She left cans of tuna out on the counter for our pride of cats. She mulched her garden with manure and blood meal. For all her beauty, I was sure she was a witch who might just be fattening me up before she tossed me into the oven.

My earliest memory is of her handing me a bowl of brown sugar lumps to suck on—to occupy me while she worked on one of her costume designs or distract me while she talked on the phone, getting out the vote for one of her political campaigns. I sat at the kitchen counter as each hard dark cluster of crystals dissolved into an intoxicating river of sweetness that flooded my mouth.

My mother laid out a cornucopia of delights for anyone who showed up at our house. Everyone was feasted, pampered, and entertained. She never said, *no, no, not now; that's too much; wait for later; you'll spoil your appetite.* She said, *there's always more; there's always enough; don't you want a little cream with that?* The berries were soaked in brandy and the cakes oozed caramel and custard. She kept chocolates and cookies in her lingerie drawer and knew we knew that's where they were hidden and never complained when we rummaged through her silk underthings to find the candied orange and the molasses crisps. Food, for my mother, was intimacy.

She nursed us all at a time when most kids got the bottle. She'd had to fight to get us to her breasts in those postwar days of new and improved baby formulas. No one told her how or that she should. She seemed to be born knowing that her body was food, that the whole world was food, that finally it all came down to eating and being eaten.

One rainy day we ventured across the canal to my grandmother's home. My father was from a working-class Irish family, and his parents had raised six kids, scrimping and saving to be able to retire at last to a tidy little shingled house on Cape Cod. My grandfather had promptly dropped dead, and my grandmother had settled into an orderly, careful old age. When we arrived that afternoon, there was a small loaf of homemade bread cooling on a rack on the counter. Beside it was a jar of my grandmother's homemade blackberry preserves. I can remember no other time when I was alone in a room with these two women—my mother and my father's mother.

Marrying my mother had been a radical act of defiance on my father's part. Not only was my mother not Catholic, but she was an upper-crust

English woman, her very background an affront to the colonial injustices my grandparents were striving to escape. On top of that, she and my father had openly lived together, unmarried, for years. When they finally tied the knot with a justice of the peace, my father's parents refused to attend the wedding. My father had married a sinner and a snob.

My mother seemed too big for my grandmother's tiny kitchen and oblivious to how uncomfortable my grandmother was with her presence in the room. I could see my grandmother evaluating my mother's too short shorts, her long bare legs, her blowsy hair, her dangly earrings. My grandmother, with her pink cardigan neatly buttoned, offered us a cup of tea and a slice of bread. She spread a skim of butter across each thin slice and added a taste of jam. She put the slices on little plates with little pink flowers and brought them over to the tiny table.

My mother ate her bread in two bites and emitted a satisfied grunt. "Oh Molly," she exclaimed. "That is divine. Divine!" Without asking permission, she stood up and went over to the counter to cut herself another slab of bread, which she smeared with the remaining butter in the dish. She spooned jam across it. "Perdita, shall I make you another?"

I shook my head. My hands were folded in my lap. I noted the spice rack with six spices above the stove, the discrete geranium in the windowsill, and the portrait of Jesus, his exposed heart wrapped in what I was sure was barbed wire. The picture both frightened and intrigued me, and I wondered about my grandmother's relationship to that anguished man. I had noticed the cross in the living room with his dead body pinned to it, the jumbled rosary beads by her bed, and every mention of her daily attendance at mass. Both my parents were uninterested in religion. They never spoke of God or prayer, forbade my grandmother from ever taking us to church, and made sure that we never spent very much time alone with her. There was something about this seemingly ordinary old lady, something secret and strange that frightened my parents.

I spent the night in her house only once, when I was very little. I dreamed of the thin sorrowful man in the painting leading me down, down beneath the ground to a vast dark cavern. From black passageways glowed the bones of skeletons who began to shake and whirl, to dance around me, their teeth chattering in their white skulls. I was immobilized with terror, sure these spectral figures were going to claim me, keep me forever in their bony embrace, never allow me to return to the land of the living, devour me for sure. I woke up clutching the thin white percale of the bedsheet and barely able to breathe as I stared into the darkness, not daring to call out to my grandmother in the next room.

I looked down at my hands and could see my own bones beneath the skin.

From that moment on I could not stop thinking about where life eventually leads us all. When would I die? How would I die? What did I need to know before I did? Even as a child these questions haunted me.

Leaning against the counter, my mother consumed a slice of still-warm bread and cut herself another. My grandmother's lips were pursed disapprovingly, but my mother didn't seem to notice.

"Molly, you've got to give me the recipe. I usually get my bread up in Cambridge. There's this bakery that does an absolutely marvelous sourdough, but this, this, fresh out of the oven, is absolutely beyond the beyond. Oh, I just can't get enough of it." My mother stuck her finger into the jam jar and scooped out a sticky dollop which she stuck into her mouth. "And these blackberries! I can't believe you made this yourself. I don't have the patience for jam."

My grandmother had gone to mass that morning and prayed to her God to give her this day her daily bread—and my mother had arrived unexpectedly, an entitled goddess from one of the old stories, and eaten it all.

I was still hungry, appalled by my mother's behavior, but equally uncomfortable with my grandmother's restrained disapproval. The few meals she had ever cooked for me had been tasteless, with portions that were much too small. The one rectangle of shredded wheat sitting in a shallow puddle of skim milk. The dry baked potato with a tiny square of yellow margarine. A single hard sucker from the dish.

"What's the matter with those people?" she once said within my earshot about somebody who was overweight. "Why can't they control themselves?"

I wanted my grandmother not to care about the jam, but she did. I wanted my mother not to finish the loaf of bread, but she already had.

What most defines the civilized human animal is a disconnection from the organic guidance of our appetites. For earlier peoples, hunter-gatherers still, their hunger led them where they needed to go. They carried little and ate whatever was available. In some seasons they gorged themselves on fruits and honeycomb, while in others they subsisted on the tough shreds of last year's jerky. Animals in the wild fatten up before the winter, but they are never chronically overweight, as long as they don't have access to human refuse. True, sometimes food is scarce, and their numbers diminish. One season is a mast year, and the forest floor is littered with acorns and hickory nuts. The next year the chipmunks, squirrels, and mice proliferate, thriving on the unexpected plenty—until, of course, the hawks and owls rebound and the vultures circle overhead. Deep in the ground, the abandoned acorns begin to sprout and grow. The Earth offers to all creatures vast cycles of abundance and scarcity that entangle us with the desires and appetites of all other creatures.

But when human beings began cultivating crops and hoarding grains in their city-states, they set themselves against these regulating rhythms of the natural world. Some people, the aristocrats, always had too much. Some people, the enslaved, never had enough. Religions arose to tell those on the bottom that hunger was holy and those on the top that their banquets were well-deserved. How many of my grandmothers, trapped in poverty and piety, learned to ignore their appetites? How many of my ancestral mothers, gold chains around their necks, were willing to eat their children to live another day?

Beneath the monuments and museums, the mausoleums and mass graves of civilization, is the deep organic wisdom of our ancestral mothers. Since civilization set itself against the rhythms of the Earth, it also set itself against the primordial womb from which all life comes—wanting to control fertility of plants and animals, seeking to defy death itself for human beings, and resisting the ever-changing creativity of nature. Religions of all kinds urged us to turn our eyes toward the purified abstractions of a singular organizing deity, instead of the many bodies of our mothers. They told us to control our gluttony and extinguish our desires, even as our souls craved a spiritual sweetness that became harder and harder to find and receive.

My grandmother may have suppressed her physical appetites, but she still knew how to satisfy her soul with morsels of real spiritual food. She often held a thin umbilical cord of beads, a rosary, that led to a washed-out mother goddess, the Mary of the modern church, but a mother nevertheless. My own mother had no such resources. For all of her lush indulgence, she also had within her a starving child, bereft and alone, frightened and forsaken. She arrived at my grandmother's house wanting to be fed in ways she didn't even understand. She longed, as so many of us do, for a mother's nurturing. But she did not know how to receive the love of a spiritual mother. Eventually she would drown the cries of that forgotten child with drink.

Along with her recipes, my mother bequeathed to me her mother hunger. For so much of my own life I reeled between ascetic denial and defeated overindulgence. In my early twenties I tried to become my grandmother, starving myself and converting to Catholicism, an indoctrination my mother instinctively knew wouldn't take. After all, the day after my baptism she sent me the money for my abortion. In any case, no one gave me the old folk practices and prayers I really wanted—just creeds and rituals of conformity that had been used to control my grandmothers through the ages. I went to Buddhist monasteries and watched my breath go in and out, let go of my thoughts, and tried to ignore a longing within me that I could not satisfy. I lived on sugar, an odd eucharist of coffee and cake, alternating fad diets and spiritual programs of one kind or another that I always, eventually, abandoned. I wanted something, and I had no idea what it was. When I had my own children, that yearning became both vaster and more insistent. I felt like I was becoming a hungry ghost, a being with a bottomless stomach and a mouth too small to ever eat what it really needed. That our devouring capitalist culture was simultaneously becoming obsessed with vampires and brain-eating zombies felt like a confirmation of how I also had begun to feel.

One day in New York City, riding the subway to a freelance writing job and looking out the dark window into the abyss of grimy tunnels winding underground beneath the concrete, I felt all around me, palpably, the souls of the dead. Not just the human dead but eons of beings—trees and ferns, fish and fowl, rats and cockroaches and pigeons, creatures of all kinds—who had lived and died and become the very bedrock of this land. I found myself calling out to them. *What is it I want? What is it I need? What is it that will really satisfy my longings?*

The answer I heard in my heart would take me on a winding journey into the depths of time and the dark mysteries of the Earth.

*"We are the answer to your longing,"* said the dead. *"The dead have always fed the living."*

Soon after, I learned my grandmother's rosary prayers without bothering anymore with doctrine or dogma. I began to ask my ancestors for help in a very private, almost embarrassed, daily practice with only the dead themselves for guidance. Our family lived in a little house in the mountains, and over the years our devotion to the oaks and the hemlocks, the hawks and the herons, the bears and the possums, even the bluestone beneath our feet, brought us back to the nourishment of the Earth itself. My husband Clark and I became recognized as devotees of the "divine feminine," but what we'd found was bigger than a singular gender and more powerful than any ideology. What we'd found, and knew we could never lose, were our mothers. All of our mothers—beneath us, before us, behind us, above us, and within us.

I was driving home from picking up my groceries during COVID when my car broke down on the narrow winding road that connected our little mountain town to the shopping center some miles away. Actually, the power steering went, and for a moment I thought I might crash. With great effort I managed to ease the vehicle onto a narrow strip of grass. I took out my phone to call for help but, of course, there was no service there.

I had driven this road for decades, often more than a couple times a week, curving around this way and that, following the twists and turns of a rock-strewn stream meandering toward the Hudson River. I had driven the kids to countless lessons, practices, and meets. I'd navigated back and forth to the hospital too many times to count when my mother lived with us before she died. I knew that road so well that I could drive it in my dreams—but until the day I broke down in front of it, I had never paid any attention to the little white church on a hill right beside where I now found myself. Worn stone steps led up through a graveyard to a statue in front of the building.

I thought I might be able to get some bars if I were on higher ground, so I got out of the car, noticing for the first time the name of the church: St. Anne's. I wasn't sure who St. Anne was but figured I might as well ask for her help with my power steering. I'd assumed the statue, encased in a concrete grotto, was of the Virgin Mary, but when I reached it, I discovered that it was of an older woman with a young girl at her side. Perhaps this was St. Anne. In any case, my phone was now getting reception, and I was able to call for a tow. I sat down on the steps to wait for the truck. I could see the road from where I was, the whole surrounding valley, the streams and rivers, the mountains behind me.

I googled St. Anne and discovered that she was the mother of the Virgin Mary. The little girl in the statue was the Madonna herself with a much bigger mother behind her. Over the years I had learned to trace the sediment of older traditions and devotions in various religious lore, so I began a deep investigation into Anne while I waited and the sun set into the mountains. As a saint she had been most popular in the Celtic countries that had retained connections to the old gods and goddesses. She had come with the Irish and the French to the Americas but traced her heritage back through Christianity to Anu, the great mother goddess of the oceans. Ancient legend had it that Charlemagne himself had discovered not only her tomb but her actual body—hidden in a cave beneath a hill.

There was still no sign of the tow truck, so I walked around the little white church. Behind it was another set of steps leading into a hemlock grove. The gravestones here were broken and untended. The trees were thick-trunked and very old. Before me, set into the ground with stones was a six-sided star, a hexagram. It was one of the strangest and most magical things I had ever come upon. I had no way to explain it.

Honking interrupted my reveries. I ran all the way down the hill to meet the repairman who was utterly mystified as to why I had called him when I turned on the car. Everything was working again. "Is there any chance the power steering will quit again?"

"Not likely," he shrugged. "But I'll follow you back to your house in case it does."

The car was fine.

Although it took me a while to recognize this ordinary miracle, Clark and I became fascinated by this odd little church which had been built by Irish immigrants who'd come to this country like my grandparents in the last century. Reading old newspaper articles, we discovered that it had become famous as a pilgrimage site, with people coming from all over to experience St. Anne's miraculous powers. Huge services were held in front of the statue, where healings were reported and all kinds of prayers were answered. St. Anne was famous for her life-giving powers, and her specialty was finding partners for her devotees and children for her children. But during Vatican

II the little church had been decommissioned as if everything happening there had become a little too far-out for the staid church fathers.

Legends had grown about a mysterious dark woman who haunted the graveyard and lived in a hidden crypt within the hill. Once, it was said, a group of boys ventured beneath the church and found a ghostly lair where the roof and walls were lined with the bones of the dead who had slipped beneath their graves deeper into the earth. The hill itself might once have been sacred to the Indigenous peoples. I could find no mention of the six-sided star, although I did later learn, on talking to the descendants of those buried in the graveyard, that the suicides had been put "out back" away from the so-called faithful out front.

My grandmother might have been out front with her religion, my mother out back with the heretics, but beneath both these women, beneath all of our mothers, is a dark cavern filled with the memories of the dead. Only when we begin to remember the dead, to remember that every mother has a mother, will our mother hunger begin to abate. That cavern is a womb that births all life, a tomb that takes life back within itself, a treasure trove of miracles waiting for each of us to recover who we really are and what our life is really for.

When my grandmother died, one of my many cousins told me that they had discovered a mason jar filled with unbroken wishbones when cleaning out her house. There were also jars of bits of wire, old buttons, tacks and nails, scraps of cloth, and other odds and ends. For a thrifty woman raising so many children during the scarcities of the Depression none of that was surprising. But the wishbones—washed and dried—were inexplicable. She had never invited one of her many grandchildren to make a wish after dinner. She had never made a wish herself. At first, this seemed impossibly sad to me, as if she had so successfully vanquished her desires that she wanted nothing at all, not even an inconsequential wish. But I couldn't let go of that jar.

What use could they possibly have had for this woman? Why didn't she just throw them away in the garden? What were those wishbones waiting for?

It felt like old magic buried so deep that my grandmother might not have even really known what she was up to, hiding away a jar full of miracles for her descendants who might have scarcities she could not yet even imagine.

My mother crunched bones after dinner. My grandmother put them into a jar. Both of their bodies now have been devoured by the earth. My mother knew how to eat, my grandmother how to die, but we must remember how to do both if we are going to truly live. Our bodily appetites and our spiritual hungers were never meant to be pulled apart.

Sometimes I imagine my mother and my grandmother in the ancestral realms screwing the lid off that jar of wishbones together, opening a portal to a realm neither was able to fully access in life but which now will let me recover, from the depths and darkness of time, the lost story of our mothers.

# A Message from the Old Ones

What we knew, which you have forgotten, is how we feed each other.

We knew how, after a mother died, to recognize her when she returned—the deer stepping into the glade and meeting our eyes, the salmon with the lithe silver body writhing in our hands, the swan spreading her wings as she landed before us, showing us her heart. "Take, eat, this is my body," the one you call Jesus will say, trying to help you remember the old ways. But you will think it is only *his* body that feeds you, only *his* body that magically transforms from flesh into bread and wine. No. No. No. We all do. We all die and come back. Every seed of grain, every grape from the vine, every goat and sheep that you eat was once your mother, your grandmother, and their mothers and grandmothers, who have loved you through vast cycles of leaving their bodies and returning to new bodies throughout deep time. These mothers and grandmothers are always ready to feed you.

When we were your mothers, we nursed you with our milk when you were born. Sometimes our sisters and our mothers and our cousins nursed you, too. Women circled you and fed you with their bodies. And when we died, our flesh became food for our other children—the hyenas and the coyotes, the worms and the beetles, the vultures and the crows. We always returned to you—reborn as deer, as salmon, as swans—to offer up our bodies to you again, so you could eat and live and give birth to children who would one day give birth to us.

We must remember that everything we eat—not just the bodies of animals, but the roots and stalks of plants, the seeds and nuts of trees, the flowering fruit of the fungi—has been our mother. Our appetites are what lead us back to forgotten mothers of all kinds. When we are eating, we are always eating the bodies of our mothers.

The spiders know this. The father offers up his body to the mother so she can nourish their young. The tree knows this. One day she falls and lets her rotting bark feed her saplings. The wolf at the back of the herd knows that the old or the lame caribou lingers for them, offering up its life for the lives of their wolf children. This is why the wild ones will never take too much. This is why they will always know how much is enough. They know how to eat because they still remember their mothers and grandmothers from all of their incarnations.

You are frightened because your people have known great hungers, terrible hungers, the horrors of the hungry. You know that when the wars have been bad and the fields have gone fallow and there is no more grain in the bin, you might eat each other. That in the bad times, you have eaten each other. You have seen the starving villagers digging up the graves in the cemeteries to devour the corpses. You call them fairy tales: the stories of the old women in the forest who will eat your children.

Rest in our arms for a moment, little one. You have known such sorrows and trials. We are not asking you to eat each other like that. Nor are we going to throw you into the oven today. No. Those are atrocities that arose precisely because you do not know how to eat and, most of all, because you do not remember how to die. You do not know how to eat because you no longer know how to be eaten.

Once upon a time, a very long time ago indeed, you trusted your mothers to feed you—and you trusted your mothers when the winters went on too long and dry times descended upon the land. You knew how to lie down upon the ground and let your body return to the womb of the Earth. You knew that other bodies awaited you. There were other lives, new ways of being on this Earth. You trusted your mothers to guide all their creatures through the mysteries of time. You watched the tides ebb and return, the moon wax and wane, the stars turn across the sky, and the sun set and rise again. You woke each morning to a new day. You were reborn after the sleep of death into a new life and a new body. All was in motion, all dancing, all rebirth and reunion.

You did not kill the children of your enemy, because they were your children. You did not fell every tree in the forest, because they were your mothers. You met the boar out in the woods and knew that she would feed you or you would feed her, but that no one would ever be lost to each other. You would not put your mother into a pen so small she could not lie down to feed her young. You would not make her wallow in her own filth as you forced her to give birth to children who you would eat without thinking of who they had been to you. You would not force the plants to always be in fruit and flower. You would not transform the entire Earth into a single banquet for a single life.

Nor would you dream of being done with this world, the mothers who are always ready to hold and love you, of abandoning the children whom you have loved throughout time.

The tree does not dream of denying itself rain to become holy. The bird does not languish without worms because it is wise. The plants and the animals know that their appetites bind them to each other. Our very hunger binds us intimately to each other's bodies, connects us to what we really want and who we really are. We can enter into a relationship with the many mothers on this Earth who are ready to feed our bodies with their own—and call forth from within us the memory that we, too, are mothers of all that is.

Souls come and go and come back. The dead long for bodies, for the sunshine on their limbs, for the dew on their tongues. The dead long for life. But the living must also cherish the dead to remember what life is really for. We are bound to each other.

Turn over a tree and see the roots tangled round each other. Peer closer and see the almost invisible threads of the fungi woven round and round the roots. Look again and see the snakes and the worms coiled and writhing in their midst. Beneath the surface of the world, in the dark mysteries of deep time, we are bound together with all that is.

Your appetite entangles you with the great mysteries of your most ancient mothers.

We remember who you have been. We know who you are. We know what feeds you, and we know whom you will feed when you are done with your body.

We are all consuming each other, feeding each other, and becoming one another—world without end, life without end, love it does not end. So be it.

## Chapter Two

# THE FAIRY GODMOTHERS

My mother could make me anything I wanted to be. As a child she transformed me into a swan, a mermaid, a white Persian cat dressed like an elegant Victorian lady with a porkpie hat and a ruffled bustle to accentuate my tail.

She'd trained as a costume designer. At a time when most of the women from her milieu were headed to the Seven Sisters to study French or literature and get a ring on their finger, she was painting nudes at the Art Students League, sleeping with handsome men poised to become actual Hollywood legends, and earning herself a spot at the Yale School of Drama's design program even though she didn't have a bachelor's degree. She could create worlds from paint and cardboard and cloth. Edith Head, who would go on to win countless Oscars for her costumes, wanted my mother to come out to LA and make movies with her. Her teachers wanted her to stay at Yale and teach. Sondheim wanted her in New York on Broadway. Everyone wanted her—but she only had eyes for my father, a handsome Boston doctor with a rough edge and an eye for beautiful things. She imagined she could make a whole different kind of world with him.

By the time I was born—her late, last child—she was living in a small New England town, volunteering with the Garden Club and the League of Women Voters. She no longer commuted to Harvard to design the Hasty Pudding Show for cross-dressing undergrads or to teach the history of fashion at Emerson College. The days of putting on medieval festivals with famous poets in Cambridge were behind her—as were, she hoped, my father's dalliances with yet another pretty wife of a famous professor.

Our home became her stage, a fantastical world where she coaxed orange and fig trees to bear fruit in our kitchen, where iguanas and boa constrictors wandered among primordial ferns in our living room, where cats were always giving birth in some upstairs closet, and the walls were decorated with giant abstract nudes tangled in ecstasy. The cupboards overflowed with cloth, ribbons, threads, paints, dyes, and watercolors. Everything you needed to make anything was readily available—everywhere you looked something was becoming something else.

But my mother's great yearly project was my Halloween costume. All of her prodigious talent went into ensuring that I would win best in show at the town parade. "What do you want to be this year?" she would ask me some drowsy summer day out in the garden, daring me to challenge her formidable skills. Sometimes she'd hand me a sketch pad, a box of colored pencils, some pastels, and tell me to draw something that she could make. Sometimes she'd send me inside to browse through her art books and her volumes on the history of costume or the picture books that filled the shelves. But mostly she asked in a slightly disinterested way and went back to whatever she was doing—mulching roses, yanking up weeds, or squishing beetles and slugs between her fingers.

Pots simmered on the stove with paella, fruit rotted in bowls next to the junk mail, and the pantry was full of old rusted cans of strange unearthly edibles—bamboo shoots and snails in sauce and lemons floating in brine. She often muttered under her breath while she worked in a strange, dissatisfied hiss, like she was the snake she had bought for my brother and often wore around her neck until it grew so large the neighbors complained and he had to be given away to a zoo.

To encourage my feats of imagination she read me books about magic: Edith Nesbit, C. S. Lewis, Edward Eager.

Children in these stories, left to their own devices, talked to the animals and the trees, time traveled, made wishes, got into no end of trouble, and eventually arrived back from their enchanted adventures with the resources they needed to fix the miseries of their mixed-up parents who no longer had access to realms of miracles and enchantment. I got the message.

Perhaps that is why, in third grade, I asked my mother to turn me into the blue fairy from *Sleeping Beauty*. I didn't want to be the princess. A pretty dress, a jeweled headband—how ordinary and uninspired and boring. No, at ten years old I wanted to be the rotund middle-aged wimple-wearing godmother who waves her wand and keeps the princess safe from the grown-ups. I didn't want the magic to happen to me: I wanted to make the magic happen. I wanted a wand. I wanted power. I didn't want to be a pretty little princess girl. I wanted to be a spell-casting force of a woman. I wanted to be my mother.

My mother never acknowledged any of this. Whatever I wanted, she made. There was no discussion or analysis or judgment. She did some sketches, cut out some patterns from old newspapers, and put me in the car to take me to the fabric warehouses outside Boston. As usual, I was left to my own devices, walking among bolts of cloth and aisles of color, running my hands along velvets and brocades, pressing my cheek against the satins and the silks. Each piece of fabric was a woven world from which other worlds could be created and stepped into. I became fascinated by weaving and embroidery, how threads went back and forth from one side to another, how a single thread entangled itself with so many other threads to make cloth, which could be sewn to other cloth and become something wondrous.

I was not my mother's apprentice in any of this. I was not expected to do any cutting or sewing. From time to time she put me on a stool in the kitchen to fit a skirt or a sleeve, instructing me not to wiggle or talk. She took her work very seriously and didn't want distractions. I daydreamed, lost in fantasies that arrived as fully formed visions of places and people beyond my ken. I began filling spiral notebooks with stories and created puppet plays that I put on for my bored classmates. More strangely, I would find myself standing somewhere—a stone archway on a family trip or a mountain field filled with azure butterflies—and know that I had already been there in my reveries.

"Keep still," my mother muttered, pins in her mouth. She was negotiating the frame for the headdress that I would wear as the blue fairy. The same as in the cartoon movie, it was enormous, almost bigger than my body. It was also heavy and uncomfortable, but I didn't let my mother know that. I accepted whatever needed to happen for her to transform me.

On Halloween my best friend was dressed as a tree, a branch cut from her family's backyard taped to her back, and I waddled down the street, barely able to move with all my heavy petticoats and balancing the enormous, pointed headdress tied under my chin. Later that night, walking down a dark street after stopping by the house of the old lady who always gave out hot doughnuts and apple cider, we ran into a crowd of egg-throwing teenage boys. Squealing, we raced toward home, running so fast we thought we might fly. Maybe we did. Maybe the wire wings covered in blue gauze strapped to my back could lift me into the air. It clearly wasn't beyond my mother. She could do anything, couldn't she? Had my mother arranged these dragons to meet the fairy on our path? I would not have put it past her, but of course, I never asked. I knew even then that for the magic to work it could not be discussed, explained, revealed.

When I finally got home, my mother was lying in bed, a mystery novel half open in her lap, a glass of bourbon on her bedside table next to the vial of Valium. She didn't ask me about who had the best candy bars or what houses we had visited. She didn't even ask me what anyone had thought, myself included, about my costume. I'd won best in show, and the event was over for the year. The winter stretched before us with dinner parties to host, movies to go to, and fights to be had with my father about this and that.

So many women like my mother channeled their creative impulses into conventional mediums. They hid their magic in small needlepoint pillows or stitched their spells into quilts. They warbled songs to ease the drudgery of housecleaning and tuned their voices to the sleepy-time cries of their tired children. They told stories that were passed down in families for generations. The author Virginia Woolf wrote a famous speculative essay about

Shakespeare's sister Judith—a young woman with all of his talent and none of his opportunities who ended her frustrated life by suicide in a roadside ditch. Gammy, my father's mother, once told me toward the very end of her life that she had dreamed of running away with a group of traveling players and becoming an actress as a teenager. Instead, she married, raised six children, tended to her numerous grandchildren, and went to mass. In her eighth decade she took a painting class, accompanied by her unmarried sister, and perhaps, at last, began to dream again of a world that might have been. I have one of her simple oil paintings of a seaside shack at the edge of a marsh. What was it to her—a pretty place or a different life? As for my other grandmother, a depressed and defeated Englishwoman, her only work of art seems to have been my mother—whom she encouraged at seventeen to lie about her age and join the Federal Theatre Project, whose art classes she arranged, whose application to Yale she encouraged. Just like the roses she coaxed into bloom, she nurtured my mother over the years, only to see her settle into a slightly more vibrant replica of her own exhausting housewifery—the clubs, the gardens, the dinner parties.

Nor is it just women who must sacrifice their creativity on the altar of industry and production. My father, the eldest son of an immigrant, felt compelled to go to medical school and become a doctor even though he had spent his undergraduate years under the mentorship of a famous poet. He told himself he would find a way to keep writing but never did. Instead he grew more and more bitter with the passing years. One Easter as we sat around the kitchen table decorating eggs, my mother grew bored and decided to paint my father instead. She had him strip to his shorts and covered him in elaborate spirals and foliage until he was no longer himself but the Green Man, that mythic figure of life and renewal, returned. He, in turn, began to decorate her with a crown of flowers and leaves as if she were his queen. By the end of the evening they had transformed each other, stepping out of ordinary misery and back into the revelries of a people long since gone from the world.

Everyone in a different age, before the drudgery of civilization, might have been an artist—painting, singing, storytelling, and dancing. One of the great myths of our stone age ancestors is that they were violent brutes dragging clubs around and grunting at each other incoherently. In fact, the archaeological evidence tells us that theirs was a culture rich in creative expression. Visiting the paleolithic caves, the art critic Sister Wendy declared, "Art never gets better than this. It gets different but it never gets better." Some of the most delicate musical instruments are tens of thousands of years old. Some of our folk and fairy tales where bears become princes and princesses become swans may be even older still.

What distinguishes these early peoples most of all, however, is that they had time to make art. Hunter-gatherers spent only a few hours each day looking for food. They had no houses to clean, no domesticated animals to care for, no crops to tend, no bosses to please, and no cities to police. Unlike their civilized descendants who would break their backs in the field from sunrise to sunset, theirs was a lifestyle conducive to creative expression. In fact, that participatory creativity may have been, for them, what life was really for. Surely there were people who preferred to play the flute with the nightingales than sculpt herds of the nearby bison—but art was not something made by an elite class for a discerning audience. It was not produced for consumers. It was a collaborative engagement with the natural world.

An echo of these lost ways persisted in small villages into the Middle Ages where much of daily life centered around elaborate feast days for which the entire community was almost perpetually preparing and enjoying. As Barbara Ehrenreich details in her remarkable book *Dancing in the Streets*, over two hundred days of the year were devoted to celebrations centered around seasonal events honoring the old gods and goddesses, often recategorized as saints. Costumes and masks were worn, gender roles reversed, and the social order upended. Everyone was a singer and a dancer in the wild revelries that ensued. The community was bound together in a shared experience of creative culture.

When I was ten, my mother, who never went to church, approached the local Episcopal priest and suggested that he involve his entire congregation in putting on a production of *Noye's Fludde*, a Benjamin Britton opera based on a medieval mystery play. They'd gotten to know each other in antiwar demonstrations, and he, surprisingly, agreed to her request. He thought it was a terrific community-building idea. It was.

The musical director at the church was thrilled. A local banker was enlisted to sing the part of Noah, and everyone who tried out, regardless of their church affiliations, was cast as something—whether a human being or one of the many animals, including not only donkeys and cows but various shellfish, mollusks, and fiddler crabs. My modern dance class, which met in the church hall, took on the role of the Flood itself, undulating menacingly up the aisles as cymbals announced the coming rain. My mother cleared off her drafting table and began elaborate set and costume designs, brought into being by the many seamstresses in the congregation. A local sailmaker and his boatbuilding buddies worked on the ark.

Whatever disagreements were ongoing in our small seaside community—and there were many—were tabled during the months of preparation and rehearsal. You'd hear people in the local grocery store singing their parts under their breath. Actual animals were brought to rehearsals for research reasons. Papier-mâché masks were constructed by the high school art students. Hidden talents were revealed.

I'm not sure who was actually left in our small village to come to the final show, unless it was family and visitors from the neighboring towns. My mother was in her element, with a row of safety pins dangling around her neck, ready at any moment to adjust a hemline or stitch up a tear. She was too busy to drink or fight with my father. Perhaps this was true in other families as well. After all, the Flood was coming.

I've always wondered how many of the people involved in that production remembered it when Hurricane Bob nearly destroyed our little town a few decades later, washing houses out to sea and sending boats careening down the main street. We are all prescient in ways more mysterious than we acknowledge. Of all the plays my mother could have suggested, that was the one she knew our town would someday need, she would need. I was living in New York at the time, and my mother was in the midst of chemotherapy. All the phone lines were down, but I finally reached the local police station. They assured me that a whole crew had gone to rescue my mother, settle her in with friends, and make sure she had access to medical care. "It's Jerry Santos," the police officer said to me. "Remember me, Perdita? I was one of Noah's foolish sons in that amazing show your mom did at the church."

The last Halloween costume my mother made for me was Anne Boleyn. On Sunday nights when I was in elementary school we would go over to sit with our ancient neighbors and watch Masterpiece Theater on their color television. That fall they were showing *The Six Wives of Henry VIII*, and I became entranced by the story of the king's second wife, who had her head cut off because she was a witch. Did she seduce the king and destroy a country, or was she a woman trapped in a role she did not want and could not escape? I read every book I could about her while my mother refashioned the blue fairy's petticoats and designed a regal Tudor garment lined in fake fur with heavy sleeves, green satin, and black velvet. I was just beginning to have breasts and the tight corset flattened my chest and pushed my nipples against my bones. That was the last year I walked in the parade, the last year I won. After that it was all sexy kittens with cute ears and sexy witches in low-cut shirts that might attract the attention of the high school boy who had become the subject of all my fantasies, the only prize I wanted anymore, not even realizing the warning I had given to myself ahead of time about what happened to girls who became too attractive and thought they might wear the crown.

To her credit, my mother didn't miss a beat. If I wanted to be a desirable teenage girl, that is what she would help me become. She took me on shopping trips, arranged makeup lessons, a perm, a subscription to *Seventeen* magazine, but it was all a losing proposition. Easy, boring, dull. She threw herself into politics, spending hours on the telephone raising money, getting out the vote, and helping the first openly gay candidate get elected to Congress. She redesigned the living room with bamboo wallpaper, which our pride of cats instantly shredded. She cooked mousses and quenelles and ever more demanding delicacies that filled the fridge. She gardened obsessively, creating walls of roses that surrounded our home with blossoms and fragrance. She woke up at dawn and went out in the early morning to mutter strange spells to them that seemed to bring each exotic hybrid into flower.

"What's your secret?"

She looked at me, as she studied one of the rosebushes climbing up the side of our house, typically distracted, vaguely appalled. "I just put them where they like to be." She pulled a beetle off a leaf and squished it between her fingers.

"But how do you know where they like to be?"

She turned to me, an expression of disdain on her face that withered my soul. Somehow I'd missed the transmission. I might speak fluent house cat, with a smattering of inbred golden retriever, but I didn't know how to talk to plants. My mother couldn't believe it: her own daughter had no idea what the plants were saying.

She would not teach me how to do this. She would offer no instruction. I don't think she even dared acknowledge what a witch she was. But that was the day I began listening and realizing that all beings were speaking to each other, just not necessarily with words we knew or languages we could study.

We could only grow quiet, immerse ourselves in their presence, and begin to accept their guidance.

I wanted to ask her who she was and if she had been planted in the right place, somehow, after all. But I never did. She interrupted my reveries.

"When I die," she said, "feed me to my roses. Ashes are heavy. Do something useful with mine. Turn me into mulch."

That moment was a long way away, and when the time came to put her in the ground, her rose gardens were all gone—sold with the house, abandoned by the new owners, forgotten even by her. But I grew because her body had been the mulch for my life, a life of magic where anything could become anything and we could all become who we already are.

# A Message from the Old Ones

Come with us down to the water's edge at twilight. We want to show you how souls come together to make a world.

The sun stipples the clouds with pink and gray, calling to the salmon in the streams. The tree frogs fill their throats with golden air and sing to each other through the trees. The purple iris holds her petals close. The beaver awakens, drawing circles that ripple across the body of the pond. A bat begins to dance in the gloaming. Each of these beings—frog and iris, bat and beaver—expresses itself in a way that is uniquely its own yet shared among all of its kind. The trees sigh, exhaling breaths of the invisible mist they have collected throughout the day. Deep in the dirt the mushrooms are preparing to burst through the earth in circles upon the ground.

Where are you in these circles, our children? What are you singing? How are you dancing? What shapes are you drawing across the body of the Earth?

A long time ago, when our blood came, we would take ourselves into the caves with the moon. There in the womb of the world we learned to make new worlds. We pressed our bloodied hands against the stone and saw, in the flickering light from our torches, the rocks come alive with the beings of our world. We left dots upon the walls to mark the days of the moon that told us when we would return to the caves. We began to create and count and conjure. We became artists in the caves, adding red ocher, the blood of the Earth, to our own blood as we created the world to which we wanted to return.

Our paintings were prayers for intimacy, for kin, for life itself. We painted the animals we loved—the mammoths, the aurochs, and the deer. We did not paint ourselves. We painted the animals we had been and wanted to be again. We painted a pride of cats racing across the plains, because we were a pride of cats, fierce, wild, and holy. Most of our art vanished in the dust of time, as we knew it would, because all things vanish into time.

We watch the spider weave her web between the trees. Pollen decorates the strands of her creation. The winds blow the web away. We watch the world always changing, always becoming something else. The ice washed away the forests. The fires renewed the flowers. The blood in our bodies did not make babies this month, so we used it to make worlds. We wasted nothing. We unraveled the threads we'd spun and spun new threads. We pulled apart the clothes of the old one who had died to stitch together the quilt for the babe who would be born. Worlds are always ending and beginning again. Nothing need ever be thrown away. Everything is always making something else. The leaves fall and become the mulch to feed the roots of another tree.

You, our dear children, are frightened now because you see the world unraveling. The insects are vanishing. The birds are vanishing. The trees are vanishing. The fish in the sea are almost gone. You have covered the world's canvas in asphalt and concrete. You have made things you think will last, enshrining your art in museums and auditoriums the way you imprison your animals in zoos. You pride yourself on your cathedrals built atop the forests you have decimated. But you throw everything away, even yourselves. What if you are not the souls who found art but lost it?

What art did you lose when you stopped collaborating with all of nature? You applaud your geniuses and virtuosos, yet you mostly sit in the audience of life. You have forgotten that each of you has within you the creations the world most needs.

But we have not forgotten. We can give you back your songs. We remember how many times the world has been erased and redrawn. Come and sing with us so that the dandelions can crack the concrete. Come and dance with us so the moss can feel at home on the stones. Let us together entice the vines up the walls to regreen the land.

Come, come to the water's edge.

The world you have known is in its twilight, but now is the time to go into the darkness and dream. Come with us into the caves and let us remember together what our blood is really for.

## Chapter Three

# MAKE LOVE NOT WAR

"What would you let a boy do to you?" Suzie was reading from a tattered piece of paper she had inherited from an older girl. "Would you let a boy put his tongue in your mouth? Would you let a boy put his tongue in your ear? In your belly button? In your . . ."

All of the girls at the seventh-grade sleepover, crowded into Suzie's tiny bedroom, squealed in horror.

"Shut up!" yelled Diana.

"No!" gasped Mary, covering her face with her hands.

"Ew!" screamed Colleen and Annie as one.

I wrinkled my nose and tried to look disgusted. I had often found myself out of step in gatherings of kids over the years. I didn't watch the same TV shows or listen to the right music or go to church on Sundays. Not only was my mother as old as most of my friends' grandmothers, but my parents dressed differently, talked differently, and ate differently than everyone in our little New England village. My mother wore silk caftans, and our house was filled with abstract art. At dinner, she served salads made of strange leaves and actual flowers. We went to plays and art museums and antiwar demonstrations instead of baseball games and barbecues. With a much older brother and sister, I grew up with the music of an earlier generation and tagged along to movies for which I was most certainly too young. No one in my family worried about it, but when I went to school, I quickly learned to pretend and behave like the other girls so I might feel like I was fitting in. "Oh yes, I love that song!" I'd lie. "My parents won't let me watch that show," I'd announce if someone mentioned a sitcom I didn't know, as if there were rules in my house, too, about what was appropriate and what was allowed. There weren't.

What would I let a boy do to me? The question alone, not to mention each escalating suggestion, made me feel breathless and tingly. By seventh grade I was obsessed with thinking about what I would let a boy—or let's be honest, anyone—do to me. I didn't have much to go on—just couples writhing discreetly under the sheets in prestige TV dramas, sometimes the flash of a bum or a boob in an art movie, and breathless descriptions in the dense historical novels that I consumed voraciously about somewhat abstract episodes of bodice-ripping ravishment.

What would I let a boy do to me? Anything. Anything at all. I wanted to be touched. I wanted hands on me. I wanted fingers and tongues slipping in and out of every orifice on my aching body. But no way was I going to admit to any of that in a room full of adolescent girls.

"I heard," whispered Mary who always knew everything, "that Barbara Cavendish let a boy put his hands down her underpants behind the bathhouse at the beach!"

Now everyone was screaming dramatically. Suzie covered her head with a pillow. "I don't want to know! I don't want to know!"

Barb Cavendish, two grades up from us, rode my bus. She got on last and sashayed down the narrow aisle while every boy turned to stare at her passing rear. Her bleached blonde hair was blown out into a waterfall of curls and waves, freckles covered her nose, her lips were red with lipstick, and she had cleavage that she showed off by always unbuttoning at least three buttons of her shirt. Once in the cafeteria in junior high she was just ahead of me in line to throw her disposable tray into the trash compactor, and I heard my social studies teacher whisper under his breath as she passed, "Holy Mother of God." Barb Cavendish was fast, and I was fascinated by her. I studied her the same way I studied the pinup girls in the dirty magazine I'd found in my father's office. The question wasn't what I would let a boy *do* to me. No, the real question was how did I get a boy to *want* to do things to me?

My slumber party buddies grew up in homes where sex was almost never mentioned. Their parents were already issuing edicts from on high about dating rules and not dressing like you wanted it and what movies they were absolutely not allowed to go to—and then my mother would put us all in the car and take us to them. In my house there was a painting that covered an entire wall that showed a nude woman with her bare legs wrapped around a naked man's behind. From her fingers were emanating a burst of stars.

I had one friend who was forbidden from wearing a bikini, so my mother showed her mother ancient Roman mosaics of women in thongs as well as images from Crete of bare-breasted women wearing almost nothing at all. "All fashion is a fad," she said, which did not change this mother's mind one bit about her daughter's attire. When my mother designed the costumes for *Kiss Me, Kate*, the high school musical I was in, she had all the boys wearing tights and codpieces covered in bows. "Why not show off what you have?" she told them.

My mother was made for the sixties. Long before flower power and the sexual revolution, she was reveling in the pleasures of her body. She lost her virginity to a "beautiful man" she worked with in the theater as a teenager who would go on to become a famous movie star. "Oh, he was gorgeous," she would sigh whenever he appeared on the television screen in some old black-and-white classic. "I'll never forget him arriving for that first rehearsal in a white linen suit, the way those pants hung off his hips. Oh my, he was delicious."

My mother was stunningly beautiful herself, but it wasn't just her physical appearance that commanded attention: it was the feeling that she wanted it. Everyone could tell. My mother liked sex. When, a few years later, I found myself in a play with the entrancing Barb Cavendish, I discovered that she too liked sex and had no need for performative displays of purity. The conversations I had with her backstage about female desire, about the joys of masturbation, about what made sex actually pleasurable were unforgettably liberating for me as a teenager. "If a boy doesn't make me feel good, I don't want anything to do with him," she told me confidently.

Still, it was clear that it wasn't what you *did* that made you a slut but what you *wanted*.

My mother disappeared into the bedroom with my father in the afternoons and locked the door—but once it was unlocked, she didn't try to hide what they'd been up to. She'd lie in bed naked for hours, reading, making phone calls, inviting me in for a chat. When it came to her body and its needs, she was completely without shame. She loved to take long leisurely baths, and once, when I was eight, she opened her legs like the old Sheila Na Gig goddesses from Ireland and showed me the secret folds of her vulva. "This is where you came from," she said matter-of-factly. "It's where we all come from. It's where your children will come from."

But my mother, surprisingly, didn't talk that much about sex. She loved a dirty joke and a naughty story, but she didn't actually explain to me how babies were made. She never talked to me about masturbation or orgasms or what I was up to with the boyfriend I eventually began hooking up with. When I was put on the pill for bad menstrual cramps, my father tried to say something about this not being a permission slip that simply made my mother laugh. She let my older siblings and me, even when I was in high school, have our partners spend the night in our bedrooms but seemed completely unconcerned, and even uninterested, in the details of our experiences. Sometimes I've wondered if it was her English upbringing that instilled a certain reticence in her about anything too personal. Ultimately, however, her unusual combination of shamelessness and privacy was, perhaps, her greatest wisdom about cultivating eros.

On the one hand, animals are shameless about their courtships—yowling and rutting in full view of everyone in the open air—but on the other, they are often modest about their actual copulations. It is rare in the wild, and takes great patience, to see birds or bears in flagrante delicto. Eagles fall from the sky in each other's embrace but conceal their passions with their feathers; dragonflies become one body above the pond; tree frogs hide their delights in the darkness of the night.

The magazine I found in my father's office created a sexual template that distanced me from my own body and how it expressed arousal. Pornography turns us all into performers, enacting roles that have nothing to do with who we really are and what we really want. It traps us in a not-so-fun house of mirrors, looking at ourselves looking at ourselves, forever out of touch with touch itself.

What would it be like to occupy our animal desires again without our human hang-ups? How did women experience their appetites in the eons before civilization sought to control and dominate their bodies? Is it even possible for us to know after so many millennia of patriarchal oppression? What was sex like before the Fall? What was sex like before we even conceived of a fall from innocence and began privileging purity over desire?

For so many millennia we have been indoctrinated to mistrust our animal instincts—our appetites and our lusts, our bestial urges. Animals occupy a world of predator and prey, hunter and hunted, unlike human beings who can enjoy the refined pleasures of affection and romance. However, it is human beings who commit the very worst sexual atrocities, goading each other into ever more terrible horrors by publicizing and proclaiming the depravities they enjoy in images that steal the very soul of those they humiliate and subjugate, always reenacting patriarchy's worst hierarchies and dominations. Civilization tells men to collect and hoard women like wheat in their granaries and currency in their bank accounts, to always want new and improved bodies to conquer and control, to defile and destroy anything they cannot have. Perhaps it is the animals that can teach us again to return to the lost pleasures of courtship, flirting, foreplay, and especially desire.

Animals and plants and fungi manifest their erotic life force in so many varied ways. There are birds that mate for life but are promiscuous when it comes to fertilizing their eggs. Some fish fluctuate genders and impregnate themselves. There are animals that die even as they copulate, others that fornicate ceaselessly, and some that simply clone themselves rather than bother with the whole messy business of sex. "Eons of evolutionary time have left their mark, creating an array of apparently nonsensical, yet somehow functional, botched systems in this ever-evolving sex-defining chaos," writes journalist Lucy Cooke in her glorious book *Bitch: On the Female of the Species.*

The natural world is ecstatically generative. It wants to replicate, propagate, and effloresce; it is nothing if not creative in satisfying its desires for reproduction. The prayer of Life is to make more life—all different kinds of life in all different ways.

In an ancient myth, the hermaphroditic seer Tiresias is asked by the gods whether men or women enjoy sex more. The prophet concludes that it is the female of the species who has the greatest sensual satisfaction. But what of other species? Who are we to say that the bird who copulates only for a moment does not know a quality of ecstasy in those unfolding instants that we can barely imagine? A bear can smell an odiferous cosmos unavailable to us; a deer can see colors beyond our ken; a bat knows how to feel the vibrations in the air. Of course, they must bring each of these sensitivities to the activity that ensures their very survival. Desire is what calls us home to who we are and who we might become.

Among bonobos, our closest primate kin, the vibrant expression of female sexuality is what keeps the community peaceful. As recounted by researcher Helen Fisher, "Sex is almost a daily pastime. . . . Bonobos engage in sex to ease tension, to stimulate sharing, to reduce stress while traveling and to reaffirm friendships during anxious reunions. [They] walk arm in arm, kiss each other's hands and feet and embrace with long, deep, tongue-intruding French kisses."

There is abundant evidence that our paleolithic ancestors' daily lives were similarly centered not around violence but pleasure, specifically female pleasure. Like our bonobo cousins, touching and cuddling and pleasing each other were daily delights. Rather than a man demanding that a woman be chaste so that he could ensure her child was "his" property, every child belonged to the clan—with both men and women perceiving themselves as caregivers, as mothers, of every child that was born. Women might copulate with a variety of men to ensure shared responsibly for the children they might conceive. In various hunter-gatherer cultures men offered, during sex, the "father milk" of their semen to a pregnant woman—to ensure the future infant's nourishment and well-being. When that child was born, many women might have nursed it, including older and younger women without children who could nevertheless still lactate. Those who chose not to bear children could still be mothers, whatever their gender, in the context of such a community. When female desire is not harnessed to proprietorial ownership, motherhood is no longer a singular biological destiny but a communal responsibility.

On the cusp of my teenage years, I felt wildly generative. I was making things—elaborate dollhouses I constructed and decorated, story collections I wrote and illustrated, theatrical events I directed and designed. If I was sometimes teased for being bookish, I responded by being smarter and funnier than my bullies. But a moment came, just before high school, when I realized that I could publish my poems in magazines, make important points at historical conferences, and win academic awards, but none of this would make me attractive to any of the teenage boys. No one asked me to slow dance at our weekend get-togethers. No one was going to make out with me down at the beach. No one would even admit to having a crush on me. I was volcanic with desire—and I was considered, by the very narrow standards of the culture at large, completely undesirable.

If women in fundamentalist systems must keep their hair and their faces hidden behind kerchiefs and burkas, women in capitalism must conceal themselves within the restrictive confines of the perfected self and the perfect body. All of it prevents us from just being ourselves—and knowing what it is we really want.

I began focusing all of my ambition, intelligence, and creativity on the singular goal of becoming a sexual object. I starved myself (the *Vogue* diet alternating skim milk and grapefruit juice); I cut my hair (and learned to use a blow-dryer and a curling iron); and, most importantly, I stopped showing off in class. ("Oh that test was hard," I giggled.) Every movie, every television show, every magazine offered me a template for how I was supposed to look, dress, flirt, and behave. I might have been a creature from another planet studying how to pass as a human female, which had nothing to do with my natural instincts. But I got a boyfriend at long last.

The smell of him, the feel of his hard abdomen under my fingers, the darkness all around us as we crammed ourselves into the back seat of his VW Bug at the end of a dirt road in the middle of the woods, the things he made me feel. We fooled around out in the dunes and tasted the sand and the salt on each other's skin. He pressed me against my locker before class and covered my neck in kisses. We snuck into the music practice rooms during lunch to sigh against each other's bodies while some kid screeched through his trumpet lesson. With his hands and his tongue, he would make me come again and again. My pleasure was his passport to satisfaction.

For a few seasons we reveled in shared bliss. My friends Suzie and Annie and Colleen were all dating his friends, and with the lights off we'd sprawl across the living room at my house, entangled in desire beneath the ferns and fig trees. We occupied a cultural sweet spot, I suppose, between the sexual hedonism of the sixties and the pornographic horrors of the internet age. We had easy access to birth control but not too much information about what we could or should be doing. We mostly discovered sex for ourselves in the darkness, by touch, guided by what felt good.

Sometimes I wonder what spells my mother had spun that made our house such a safe place for those explorations. Was it the smell of wet dirt and sweet perfume from the indoor gardenias and orange trees or the general fecundity of the ever-proliferating cats? She offered an erotic sanctuary to couples of all kinds, to her friends who were unmarried or gay or trans and who wanted somewhere to go and relax with their lovers. She welcomed everyone into her home. She'd get up early and squeeze fresh juice for whoever showed up in the morning. But I suppose most of the protective magic emanated from her own ecstasies, because once my father renounced her and her charms, leaving her for a stolid woman whose only other virtue seemed to be youth, the ordinary horrors of "civilized" sex penetrated the enchanted realm my mother had so carefully cultivated.

One of our neighbors was raped. A cousin needed an abortion. My boyfriend slept with each of my friends in turn. An older teacher began asking me over to his house supposedly to read me poetry. My friends called me a slut after I made out with the cool quarterback at a party. A coach at the high school lured another cheerleader into his office and groped her. A young man close to our family, abused by a priest, committed suicide. A girl I barely knew confided in me about the sexual violence she had endured as a child. The gay teacher at the local boarding school, my mother's best friend, was outed and fired.

What would you let a boy do to you? Would you let him rape you, abuse you, hurt you, fill you with poison, take what he wants and leave you in the trash when he is done? We were always asking the wrong questions. We shouldn't have been focused on what boys desired but on what *we* really wanted.

What do we want—truly, madly, deeply, with our whole body, with our whole being, lifetime upon lifetime? Our bodily desires, if we can uncover and claim them, can lead us to the deepest guidance of our hearts.

My mother's favorite book, which she read to us again and again, was *The Lion, The Witch and The Wardrobe* by C. S. Lewis. She had absolutely no interest in any of its Christian theology and never bothered to point out any of its religious symbolism. She loved the cozy teas with the gossipy faun, the chatty beavers and grumpy dwarves, and most of all, the lion. She would remember how she had once enticed a willing zookeeper to let her hold a lion cub and the feel of its power on her lap. "It's paws! So golden!" she enthused. She would tell me how much she wanted to ride a lion, to romp with him through the forest, to bury her face in his rough golden mane like the girls do in the story.

But Lewis would never have let my mother into Narnia. With her dark hair, towering magnificence, and imperious beauty, she could have been his model for Jadis, the White Queen, the witch herself, his slutty stand-in for Satan: the evil woman and seductress. She'd wave her wand, or her cooking spoon, serving you up Turkish Delight, and then freeze you into stone with her scorn. It was her fault that the seasons had stopped and the land was always covered in snow and ice.

Good Christian convert that he was, Lewis blamed everything on a woman. But the pagan in him, the scholar who had studied the old legends and tales and written a book about courtly love and the sacred romance, must have known he was missing something about enchantment, forgetting the primal power of the Lady and her lion. After all, in an earlier book he wrote for grown-ups, *That Hideous Strength*, the whole world is healed when the goddess Isis returns with her wild tiger at her side to wed King Arthur. The powers of Evil—depicted as a disembodied head, a kind of Silicon Valley tech bro who has uploaded his consciousness to the cloud, leveled the ancient forests, and initiated the apocalypse—are defeated by the erotic joy of the Lady and her Lord whose embodied love brings the whole world back into bloom.

One book later, however, Lewis has become terrified of feminine power, imagining it unsuitable for children. Isis is now the thinly disguised Jadis, and instead of romping with her big cat, she battles him. Instead of the disembodied male ego causing the downfall of the planet, a woman's out-of-control desires are somehow the problem—as they have been since Eve.

Rejected by my father, my mother retreated into conventionality. She put on a cardigan and joined the Ladies Committee at a local museum—organizing teas, arranging flowers, and showing tourists beautiful works of art collected from around the world by esteemed Boston patriarchs.

My mother, herself a work of art, some great fertility goddess of yore, never took anyone into her bed again. I wanted her to remarry or take a lover. But even more upsetting than her abandonment of sex was that she seemed to have renounced her very life force along with it. I wanted her to reclaim the career she had abandoned, the full artistic potential that was within her. I wanted her to feel passionate about something, anything. In retrospect, I would have been happy if she had become wilder and stranger, convening a coven of old hags at our house to concoct potions and mischief. I wanted her to *want* something—something deeper, bigger, and wilder than just another drink at the end of the day. Instead, she slowly withered and faded. Cancer came first, then long brutal rounds of chemotherapy and radiation, and eventually dementia and, not surprisingly, heart failure. She died, however, of a small bowel obstruction . . .

She'd been visiting my brother when she collapsed in the car on the way to another doctor. He rushed her to the nearest emergency room, but the doctors told us there wasn't much they could do. They inserted tubing through her nose into her stomach to reactivate her digestive tract, a torturous process, but my mother had slipped into a coma from which she would never awaken. I held her as she took her last breaths, my head pressed to her breast, heartbroken, grateful, inconsolable. The full moon, shining right in through her window, cast a pale silver light on her face as she passed. I was so angry at her during her decline without any awareness of what it was that left me flailing through my twenties feeling so alone and infuriated. I didn't understand that what I wanted from her was the implicit permission to claim and trust my own passions. I had lost myself trying to be desirable, and I no longer knew what I desired. And when we don't know what we want, we don't really know who we are. I was frustrated and furious, and perversely, that somehow became another verdict on all that my mother had lost—her beauty, her husband, her children, all of it. Women were destined to grow old, alone and abandoned. What else could they expect?

I once asked my mother what she thought happened when we died, and she looked up from her dessert, one of the few pleasures still left to her, and squinted at me, both appalled and confused. "What?"

"Do you believe in heaven or some kind of afterlife or reincarnation?"

She sighed wearily. "When you're dead, you're dead. That's it. You're dead."

"But," I began futilely. "I mean . . . you . . . your essence . . . your soul . . ."

"Oh, Perdita," she shrugged. "Give it a rest."

Yet when she was dead, she finally answered me.

We filled her coffin with roses before we placed it in the crematorium. At the last moment I took one long-stemmed blossom from her cold hands to bring home with me to press between the pages of a book, to know it was an object that had touched her body before her body was nothing but ash. After the cremation, there was a service and a reception and an exhausting drive back home. I was so tired and forsaken I just left the rose on the counter. When you are dead, you are dead, right? In the morning when I came downstairs, I saw that the base of the long green stem of the greenhouse rose had sprouted a tangle of white roots. Overnight.

How many cut roses had I stuck in vases over the years? I'd never seen anything like it. Superstitiously, I thought I had to plant the rose, get it to grow into a bush again in order to keep my mother alive. I consulted with experts at the local gardening club, none of whom had ever heard of such a thing. I read forums online and finally concocted a plan for coaxing the stem to grow. Only it didn't work. The roots withered. The rose died—and it felt like my mother had died all over again. But the messages the dead send to us from beyond the grave are often like that, vanishing like mist just after we receive them.

My mother's magic could still make things grow wherever she was.

That was when I first began to understand how powers we relinquished in life might return to us from the other side. That is when I realized how much the dead must long to be reborn, how much they must want everything to grow and blossom, root and seed. It is only the living who imagine the dead want extinction . . . the dead themselves want bodies again, smells again, touch again, love again, the blessed entanglement of cocreation. And in order to be reborn, they need bodies to incarnate into . . . and those bodies need love and passion.

Isis, the great mother goddess, resurrects her murdered and dismembered husband Osiris explicitly to have sex with him and impregnate herself. The ancient Egyptians created phalluses made of clay and seeds that would flower on their feast day in tribute to their love. Osiris is both the lord of the dead and the god of the living because of this. Inanna and Dumuzi, Ariadne and Dionysus—the story of lovers bringing the world into bloom is older than religion and at the heart of it. Mary Magdalene invokes this ancient ritual when she identifies the resurrected Jesus as the "gardener" come back to plant his seed within her and renew the world. Sex in all of its expressions and varieties is the magic at the heart of the world.

When my father died, ten years after my mother, I was fully into menopause and had not menstruated in over eighteen months. But the day after his funeral I began to bleed, and I got my period, regularly, for six months afterward. I knew my father was asking to be reborn into our family—but he would have to find another way back into the world. Clark and I didn't want any more babies by then. We were too busy writing books together.

That I was with a man who desired my desire—for family, for love, for writing, for the Earth—was its own kind of miracle. We lived together in a little run-down house in the mountains filled with plants and animals and children. Somehow, despite losing touch with my own yearnings in my twenties through wrongheaded relationships of all kinds and jobs I didn't love, I was with someone for whom the erotic and the spiritual were one and the same. Our cars were always breaking down and the roof was always leaking. We often didn't know how we were going to pay the bills, and we could fight with transcendent fury. But everything could be made whole and healed in each other's arms. We knew how to bring each other into bloom.

The fact that young people are having less sex than ever before should concern us. Eros is life force, and without life force, life cannot renew itself. That middle-aged and old people are not having joyous sex should concern us. The erotic is what binds us to all that is. The birds, the turtles, the trees, and the frogs—the whole world is struggling against civilization's extinction instinct, singing to renew itself, continue itself, and drive the green wick of the world through the asphalt and the concrete. We must join forces with them with our very bodies.

When my husband's grandmother turned one hundred, the whole family assembled in her house for a party. At one point she told her great-granddaughters that they could go into her closet and take whatever cashmere sweaters appealed to them. When they did, they also found a book open on her bedside table to "Supercharge Your Orgasm." That weekend, everyone kept asking this old woman what her longevity secret really was—it seems to have been an open book beside her bed.

The dead want to renew the life within themselves and within us. They want us to embrace healing and love, passion and desire. They want the great efflorescence of life on this planet to come into bloom. Let us align our prayers with theirs and let the god of the dead become again the god of eros.

# A Message from the Old Ones

Begin by asking each soul you meet in the world, "What do you want? What do you truly, madly, deeply want? What seeds are in your heart that want to sprout and grow and bloom?"

Ask the mountain about its desires. Ask the stone on the path beneath your feet. Ask the laurel after it has bloomed. Ask the salamander sitting on the wet moss. Ask the ghost pipe emerging from last autumn's leaves. Ask the hawk circling above you. Ask the clouds and the coming storm. Ask the rain. What is it that you want? What desire have you carried in your heart for lifetimes upon lifetimes? Even now, what are your prayers?

Ask and listen to the heartbeat of the world.

What is the Earth praying for?

Are the trees praying to be pure? Do the crows aspire to celibacy? Does the dandelion long to be ascetic?

When we open our hearts to the heart of the world, we hear a song of desire. The mountain longs for the touch of the rain on its body. The rain longs to sink into the body of the mountain. The mourning dove sings for a mate. The buck steps into a field for love. The salmon swims upstream for its progeny. The tree is dropping its acorns into the ground because it wants more trees. Life prays for life—and life grows from desire and love. The whole world is praying for love.

When we pray from within our hearts for all that our hearts long for, for all that our bodies want, for what our souls yearn for, we find ourselves carried in that river of love toward an ocean of love that is always calling forth life from the world.

But you, our beloved children, so lost and confused, will not find your way back to your hearts and your bodies until you can align with the life-renewing desires of all that is.

We, the grandmothers, have always cared about the ways of love. We want to hold in our arms the babes who will become our mothers when we ourselves return to life. We want to know that life goes on. We want to watch the young ones slip off into the darkness, sly smiles on their faces. We want to see our sons and daughters safe and wild in their pleasures. We want each of you to know the healing wisdom of your own body. But we cannot give you ten steps to improve your sex lives. We cannot give you a manual, a set of diagrams, a foolproof program for love. Whatever advice we might have to offer, it would become distorted and perverted by civilization's relentless lust for supremacy.

A long time ago, when people decided they were something other than the beasts, they took the simplest of joys and turned it into the most violent of pursuits. People have been hurting each other's bodies for so long in the name of love. You have been so indoctrinated into the hierarchies of submission and domination, so worried about who is on top and who is on the bottom, that you cannot easily return to the effortless pleasures of your ancestors.

If we could, we would swaddle you and hold you for a very long time indeed, singing to you in the darkness the old lullabies that we learned from the stars. We want you to feel safe again in our arms, to know that your every cry will be answered—with the milk from our breasts, with the caress of our hands, with the soothing beat of our hearts against yours. How many lifetimes has it been since you received the love that you have always needed?

We invite you to take off your shoes and step outside on the ground and feel the dirt beneath your feet. That dirt is the bodies of your ancestors. Crumble it in your fingers and know it comes from the bodies of insects and flowers and trees and stones that have died to give you a place to root and grow. These beings did not fear their desires but knew how to accept their guidance to renew the world. Draw forth all that you need to heal from the body of the Earth.

Held in the gentle embrace of our care, you will slowly remember how to eat again, how to sleep and dream again, how to move across the land and feel the guidance of the earth beneath your feet again. You will remember how to speak with the trees and birds and clouds and breeze. The frogs will teach you their love songs. The fireflies will show you how to dance for your beloved. The wind will offer its lessons on touch. Only when you have recovered the easy experience of your own body, close to other bodies that nourish and protect you, will you be able to recognize your own desires. Before you can recover the old ways of making love, you must first feel loved by all that is.

# An Invitation: You Are Circled by Mothers

Imagine that we are circled by mothers—not one mother, not one biological singularity, but many orbits of motherhood that include all those who have held us for more lifetimes than we can possibly remember. Let us summon the many beings who have brooded over our eggs, dropped us into the soil to grow, and held us in their wombs. Let us call upon the soul kin—young and old, male and female—that have nourished us, cherished us, and celebrated us. Let us summon all of our mothers.

## *Our Animal Mothers*

We begin by calling forth our animal mothers as our first protective pantheon. We begin with our animal mothers so that we can return to the animal body of our own being.

- What animals are calling to you? Do you dream of bears and owls? Or whales and dragonflies?

- Do you want an otter mother to play with you and make you feel silly again? Do you want a spider mother to help you with your writing? Do you want a bird mother to teach you how to fly? Who are the mothers you need right now? Perhaps you need a mother who is soft and gentle. Perhaps you need a mother who is small and direct. Perhaps you need a mother who can protect you with her venom and her power. Who are the mothers you want?

- Perhaps these are mothers from lives you have lived before—lives as a raccoon, a raven, or a turtle. Perhaps these are mothers from lives you are already praying yourself toward—lives as a butterfly, a seagull, or a salamander.

When we feel ourselves circled by our animal mothers, we can make space for them in our lives.

- Collect images and pictures of these mothers to remind you of their bodies. Find photos of tiger mothers with their cubs, possum mothers with their babies on their backs, goose mothers with their goslings under their wings. Feathers may come to you on your daily walk from the mothers above. A statue or a painting of one of your creaturely mothers may turn up at a thrift shop or a yard sale. A stone may look like a wolf or a fish. You may find the bone of a mouse or the antler of a deer. You may also want to create your own pictures, embroideries, or paintings of your mothers.

- Create an altar to your mothers, a place for them to gather in your home. Maybe you want to see them from your bed so when you are anxious at night you can know that they are there, watching over you. Do what feels easiest and gives your heart the greatest joy.

- Spend time with these mothers. Remember to call and say hello. Offer them flowers; light them a candle; share a bit of food with them from time to time; give them some spirits. They are always with you, circling you, there for you. We must always remind ourselves of this truth. These mothers are ready to offer us blessings and gifts and to collaborate with us to create the life we want to be living.

## *Our Earth Mothers*

Our vegetal and material mothers are also waiting for us to remember them. They are waiting to guide us home to the earth.

- We can call upon river mothers and mountain mothers. We can call on the flowers as our mothers. We can call upon the stones. Look up at the sky and know that it is the mantle of one of our mother's vibrant cloaks. Look down at our feet and know that the ground is our mother's body. Drink water from a spring and know this life-giving water is flowing from the bosom of our mother. Know that every tree and every mountain and every river is also our mother. Remember that the whole Earth is our mother.

- People sometimes recognize the shape of the Virgin Mary in the bark of a tree or the discolorations of a rock because their hearts know that the trees and the rocks are our mothers. Let us find the tree in our neighborhood that is our mother. Let us walk up a mountain path and know the mountain is our mother. Let us immerse ourselves in the ocean and feel the waters of our mother holding us up. Let us find a shell on the shore and remember that shell was once our mother.

- Let us go out on a dark night and find our many mothers. The moon is our mother, but so are the planets and the stars and the dark spaces between worlds. Each of these mothers has different wisdom and guidance for us.

## *Making Our Mothers Real*

We will know that each of these mothers is real when we cry out to them and then receive their response. But first we must call for help. Our earth mothers are here to assist us in remembering who we really are. They can help us eat, dream, imagine, and love. There are no limits on what they can do.

- Their messages may be very quiet at first: a small sign that only we will recognize, a decal on a bumper sticker, a passing reference in a conversation, a fleeting dream before waking. Slowly we will learn to accept whatever confirmation we receive. It is not proof that we can offer to anyone else about the reality of these mothers—it is a truth that we can hold in our hearts that transforms our lives. Slowly we will build an unshakable foundation of faith.

- We may find that the beasts and beings of our world begin to behave differently around us. A wren circles our head on the deck and the next day sings to us outside our window. A fox keeps crossing our path at twilight. The night is full of clouds, but just as we step outside, the moon bursts forth bright and full. Or we look up and see a particular star. Or one shoots across the darkness just as we give voice to our worries.

- Let us feel the bodies of these beings within our own bodies. Let us become mountains to become intimate with our mountain mothers. Let us know that the tides rise and fall in our own bodies like the ocean. Let us spread our wings when we need, retract our claws if we have to, show our teeth when there is danger, feel the power in our paws. Let us remember the power and possibilities in our own bodies through the bodies of all of our many mothers.

Our ancestral mothers are waiting for us to remember them. They are waiting to guide us home to the earth.

## *The Stories of Our Many Mothers*

If your mother were an animal, what kind of animal would she be? Describe your mother as the animal she is or was and what that has meant for you as her child.

> *An elephant seal nurses her pups for only a few weeks before leaving her young to fend for themselves. During their brief time together, she sings to her pup to create an unshakable bond between them—before she takes a breath she can hold for hours and dives thousands of feet into the ocean's depths. My Mum was a singer and prided herself on her controlled breathing. She was uncomfortable with children and preferred diving into her music. It took me a long time to realize that I didn't really need her on land—but underwater where my soul understands.*
>
> **—LINDA**

> *My mother was a big-bellied traveler, a relentless life-giver, a cycle keeper, a salmon. She swam above the shape-shifting shells and pebbles of her ancestors. Her strong fins carried her toward her death. She never traveled with her children, left me much too soon, but sometimes I dream that when she is a salmon again, I will be the water that carries her where she wants to go.*
>
> **—COURTNEY**

> *My mother was an independent hunter who liked to be up all night. A night nurse first, then a journalist typing into the wee hours, finally an activist stirring everyone up. She was a cat, fierce in her love, protective of her kittens with a deep purr to soothe them when they needed it, but also sharp claws and a readiness to fight for what she believed in. She was always on the prowl.*
>
> **—LAURA**

*My mother was a deer. She did the dishes by hand every day, listening to the radio and staring at a simple drawing she'd put above the sink of a doe. After her death, looking at this familiar picture from my childhood, I realized for the first time that my mother has been staring into her own soul, so gentle, so timid, always standing at the edge of a field. She hid from life but her words to me were always so kind and her eyes, looking at me, were bottomless with love.*

—**SARAH**

*No one wants to cross a gorilla. They are big and hairy and scary. My mother was not soft or safe, but she was protective. She was also quiet and private. Sometimes I wonder what kind of gorilla she would have been if she hadn't been in a zoo. She was so trapped.*

—**CORAL**

*My mother was a goat—stubborn and strong-willed, her heels dug in, standing her ground. She loved kids and let them climb on her and fix her hair, put eye shadow on her. Once she even allowed my daughter to deliver a teddy bear baby when my daughter said, "Spread your legs." Her last words during life were "I have kissable lips."*

—**ERICA**

*She's absolutely tiny, my mother, a chihuahua, but, boy, does she have a lot to say! She's fierce, she's sharp, she's loyal, and she raised a giant litter of daughters and kept us all laughing despite everything.*

—**PATTY**

*My mother was a bird who taught me to fly. Her touch was soft, feathery. Her wings would waft over my shoulders, and off she would go again, searching for more food for us. I would hear her call out "t'wee, t'wee," and I struggled to return her song. This morning, on my walk, she appeared beside me, unafraid, hopping from bush to bush and calling out to me, "t'wee, t'wee." We walked along together; she had flown through the realms to be with me.*

**—MARY**

*The praying mantis with her long torso, lanky arms, and long legs towers above most in the insect kingdom just like my mother. She was over six feet tall, could hold a basketball in the palm of her hand, and was the first woman invited to play for the Women's National Basketball League. Back in the fifties that was no small feat. She was big in stature, but her movements were graceful. She was also devout, not religiously, but to the people who mattered to her. Sadly, though, my mother's love for others did not mean she loved herself. Her hands reached for a martini or a cigarette more than for relief from the predators all around her. I wish she had prayed for herself more, much more.*

**—CHANDRA**

THE SECOND PART

# OUR MOTHERS *within* PATRIARCHY

## Chapter Four

# THE STORIES WE TELL, THE CURSES WE UNDO

I don't remember my mother's mother very well. For most of my childhood, she was a gray ghost—her gray hair coiffed into tight curls, her gray tweed suits rough to the touch, her eyes gray, her soul gray. She lived in a little gray shingled house out on Long Island that was filled with uncomfortable furniture and things that might too easily break. When I was seven, she suffered a series of strokes that left her paralyzed on her right side, bedridden and helpless. My mother moved her to a nursing home close to where we lived, built on an island in the middle of a lake that could only be reached over a narrow causeway across a great expanse of water.

My mother drove to see her just about every day, and I often went with her after school. Granny, which is what I was told to call her but never did because I never spoke to her, lay in her hospital bed, her red-rimmed eyes staring out the window. My mother watered the plants and refreshed the flowers in the vase. We often brought her stuffed animals, and my mother would tuck a teddy bear under her arm and coo, "Isn't he the sweetest?" And my grandmother might lift a finger or two and drop it down on the plush fur, never smiling. She never smiled. I sat on the floor reading a book about dragons or mermaids, absorbing disappointment and sorrow I could not fathom.

We all begin our lives within our grandmother's bodies. The egg that will become our body is already nestled within the egg that will become our mother's body within our grandmothers' bodies. We are all held within the bodies of our mothers and our grandmothers like nesting dolls. Leonardo da Vinci once painted the Madonna holding her baby and sitting on the lap of her mother, St. Anne. The grandmother is a great brown benevolent throne for her daughter, who is turning to catch her playful child. The child is reaching up their arms toward their grandmother. The lines of the painting turn in circles of belonging and connection. We are all holding each other in great mysterious circles.

But what does it mean when our grandmothers, and their grandmothers before them, are neither thrones from which we can claim our power nor laps on which we find comfort but instead are bottomless sinkholes of trauma and tragedy?

My grandmother was a chronic depressive who had been shuttled from one mental hospital to another by her children, who was plunged into ice baths and shocked with electricity—none of which could touch her morbid despondency.

With heavy sighs as we drove across the narrow road to the nursing home, water around us on every side, my mother tried to explain the burdens that women in our family carried to me. She'd been taking care of her mother her whole life. Her grandmother had been a depressive, too, she told me, who could not recover from the death of her young son. My grandmother, the child who lived, had felt responsible for her mother's unhappiness. I knew, without it being said, that my mother also felt responsible for her mother's miseries.

"It all began with postpartum depression," my mother said aloud in the car, more to herself than to me, so small I could barely see above the dashboard. "She just wasn't meant to be a mother. It was too much for her." My mother's hands tightened on the steering wheel. "I don't know. She was too attached to her own mother. Too close. That was what did her in." She sighed again. Did we drive every day to see my grandmother because my mother was also too close to her mother? Was I too close to my mother? What did that even mean?

There was only a thin guardrail between the car and the water, and I often wondered on the way to my grandmother's what would happen if my mother accidentally swerved off the causeway and we plunged into the depths of the lake. There was a primal panic deep within me on those drives that I could hardly acknowledge. One day I would drown in the hopelessness that was all around me, that had consumed all the women who came before me. My mother's sorrows were nested inside my grandmother's sorrows inside my great-grandmother's sorrows. It was sorrow all the way down.

The stories we are told as children shape our realities. *The mothers in this family are tough and can overcome anything. Your grandmothers knew how to be happy within the confines of their restricted lives. You come from a long line of women defeated by the world.* As a wider culture, too, we tell stories about who our mothers are and who they can be. "Why are the women in the children's tales always monsters or dead?" a young mother once asked me at a talk. Bambi's mother is murdered. The sleeping beauty Aurora, in order to be safe from her destiny, must be taken from her mother as an infant. Every fairy tale has a witch, a sea monster, or an ogress. Every problem we have can be traced back and back to the problems our ancestral mothers bequeathed to us—starting with Eve eating her apple and Pandora opening her box.

No wonder so many women, myself included, grow up taking our bearings from our fathers instead. "My father was a very sexual man," my mother told me at some point. "But my mother didn't like sex, and that's why my father left her." In order to avoid replicating my grandmother's failures, my mother emulated her handsome father's potency and charisma. Yet, terrifyingly to me, for all her Technicolor charms my mother was also abandoned by her husband for another woman. I was seventeen when my father left and my mother went to bed and didn't get out of it for two years. When she finally did, she made sure the liquor cabinet was always stocked with cheap bourbon. She never needed to be hospitalized for depression, but the rest of her life was a boozy haze of self-pitying resentments. "We all end up alone,

alone, alone," I would hear her moaning to herself in the middle of the night, a mournful oracle offering up a prophecy to me I did not want to hear.

When I left home, I was determined to make my life as different from my mother's and grandmother's as I possibly could—academically, spiritually, practically.

The paradox of every curse, however, is that the harder we pull against it, the more tightly it ensnares us. The more I ran from my mother, the more motherless I felt, the more I felt just as defeated and isolated as she had been from her mother. "You are just like your father," she hissed at me one drunken night over dinner when I tried to talk about our relationship. All she heard me saying was that I wanted her to change. "You don't want anything to do with me, do you? Well, let me tell you, you don't have a clue what I've endured."

Eventually, I ended up mothering her, taking care of her in her old age. She became confused and demented and was no longer capable of managing her medicine or her meals. Because I had borne witness to the daily care she had offered my grandmother, I knew I had to bring her to live with us. I had two young children . . . what was another? That felt like the curse—we all ended up mothering our mothers, never getting the mothering we craved. Would such a fate befall my own daughter?

After my mother's death I plunged into a terrible depression at all that was unresolved between us, at all that I'd always wanted and felt like I never got. I felt so unmothered. How could I possibly give my children what I had never had? I could still function, unlike my grandmother; I didn't drink like my mother; but I began self-medicating with sugar, a little something sweet here and there to help me make it through another day. I put on weight and consoled myself that I wasn't tormenting my daughter with my vanity. But in truth I felt self-pity rising within me and beginning to crush my spirit.

One rainy afternoon, I began reorganizing the hall closet and realized that in the angst of moving my mother into our home I had shoved an old steamer trunk of hers into the cobwebbed darkness under the stairs. I opened it up and found it packed with old letters in faded handwriting, antique birthday cards, and black-and-white photos of people I could not identify. Sorting through it all felt like yet another burden on my list of so many things to do. I pushed the trunk into the corner. But just before I shut the lid, I noticed a small blue book with the label *1913*. "Lest we forget" was engraved on the front cover in gold lettering. I opened the diary. In her Victorian penmanship, my grandmother had recorded what had happened to her on each day of that year.

**January 13**

> *"Awoke to white hills as there had been heavy snow in the night so I let myself have a lazy day writing letters to old friends. I still felt a bit tired after yesterday's walk."*

**May 4**

> *"A lovely day! We set off with all the cousins and walked three miles through the woods to Liddlescombe. The bluebells and primroses and violets were exquisite. We ate lunch together under an old beech on a stone bench and took the train home with flowers woven into our hair."*

**July 19**

> *"A fine evening glow after such a perfect day. We walked through blue carpets of wildflowers up the mountain after rising early, Mater and Pater taking so many photos, and took our tea later with Mildred and her husband and the Drews. I picked a rose after we walked back to the village. It is the same color as the sunset."*

I felt like I was meeting my grandmother Nellie for the very first time. I began rummaging through the steamer trunk and pulling out more and more yearly diaries. Each one was dated—1908, 1917, 1929, 1933, 1944—and each day she had recorded a few simple facts about her activities—a cooking class, a visit to the theater, and lots of walking out in nature. She was not one to talk about her feelings or analyze her actions or muse about much of anything. She was mostly matter-of-fact in noting a few details about the day. Yet she was also meticulous in her observations about the weather—from drizzles to downpours, from days of sun to days of gloom and darkness. "Clouds again today. Nothing else."

Here was a woman I'd always been told had a dull inner life and few imaginal resources. Yet day after day, year after year, she had persisted in noting the weather and some fact about each day. Perhaps because my husband was a haiku poet who carried around small notebooks in which he jotted down observations about the natural world—the bee falling into the blossom, the fireflies above the pond—I had a nagging sensation that something else was going on in my grandmother's diaries, something real and even spiritual beneath the everyday banality.

Eventually I pulled all the diaries out of the trunk and arranged them in rows by year. I sat down and began reading them in order, diary by diary, following my grandmother from girlhood to old age.

Slowly, unexpectedly, small detail by small detail, not only did Nellie herself begin to emerge more fully as a person, but her whole world began to come to life. She met her cousin to buy lace for the upcoming party. There were charades after dinner over the weekend. She took her cooking class seriously, jotting down recipes and making notes about substitutions. Her teenage years bustled with cozy routines, beloved dogs to walk, trips to the countryside with her parents and her many cousins. Like most Edwardian ladies she spent lots of time with her family.

She and her father loved to hike together, and one summer they went to Switzerland to explore the Alps along with their extended network of relatives, who were now familiar to me as I read. She did not seem at all depressed. Instead, I discovered a cheerful, optimistic young woman delighted by the world around her—the new wildflowers she was discovering, the birdsongs she was hearing, the crispness of the air in the morning.

Certainly, she was privileged. Her father was a "gentleman," which meant, I think, that there was some kind of trust fund, a little banking, and not much work. There was a cook and a housemaid. But I also found out that her father was a Fabian, one of the early socialists in Britain, and counted among his friends other forward thinkers including Arthur Conan Doyle, the inventor of Sherlock Holmes. I also knew that Conan Doyle, who was their neighbor in the countryside, was a great believer in fairies, a spiritualist open to the possibilities of the unseen world. The great children's book writer Edith Nesbit, whose stories about magical adventures influenced generations of writers from C. S. Lewis to Edward Eager, was another member of their rather progressive crowd. That my mother had raised me on these books was no accident after all—but part of her heritage, part of what was almost the secret spiritual tradition of her English mother.

Nellie never wrote about religion or seemed at all concerned with the state of her soul. But her attention to the weather—the small rain cloud off in the distance, the sudden burst of sun at the end of a walk—felt like its own devotion to wonder, as if instead of picking an oracle card each morning she simply asked the sky what it had to tell her.

In early August of 1914 while Nellie was in Switzerland, the Germans invaded Belgium. Instead of descriptions of idyllic waterfalls and charming villages, Nellie started writing about invasions, battles, and politics—and how her family was going to make their way home through an ever-expanding war zone. They quickly packed up their things and got on the first train. But the rail lines were blown up and they had to disembark at the border. Nellie saw spies being shot out near the depot. There were rumors of atrocities being committed by the soldiers. The men huddled together trying to come up with a plan of escape—when a dashingly handsome young American, a Rhodes scholar who had also been on vacation in the mountains, stepped forward and offered to guide all these British families to safety. He bribed an official, got them on another train, and eventually secured them passage on a boat back home to England. Along the way, Mr. Havens became, in Nellie's diary, Valentine, although it was hard to tell whether she was more in love with him or the excitement of the whole thrilling adventure. When they got back to London, he proposed. But she demurred.

Instead, she signed up to be a nurse, and Mr. Havens returned to America for the duration of the war.

What was it like for this sheltered young woman to suddenly find herself thrust into the middle of horrors heretofore unimaginable to most people? The first air raids. Gas attacks. Trench warfare. She is too busy to write much anymore, and every young man she knows is dying. Her cousin Ivo has the top of his head blown off and is left to perish in a rat-filled trench—but the maggots eat away at his rotted flesh and he somehow survives, a shadow of his former self. Young men she has gone to dances with lose their limbs, lose their minds, lose their lives. She has never seen a man naked before—but now she unwraps bloody bandages and washes bodies broken apart by shrapnel and disease.

Yet none of this depresses her. She is invigorated, purposeful, and alive. She had never had the opportunity to pursue a career, or even an education, and now she finds herself engaged in meaningful work each day. She falls in love with a veterinarian, stationed on the front lines with the horses. I imagine her envisioning how her new skills will support her future husband's career. Does she daydream about their life together in a little rural village with a house full of animals, tending to the local livestock? She will assist him in surgery, and they will drive out to farms together on house calls. They will spend a month at the ocean with her parents every summer—and maybe her parents will come and live with them when they get older. Her children will play together with the children of her cousins, just as she did, and she will read them all stories about fairies and magic and wishes that almost always come true. There will be afternoon walks and lazy teas and flowers in their hair again. But in the early months of 1918 her veterinarian is killed in battle.

Whatever she wrote and felt in the months following is a mystery—that is the only year that is missing from decades of diary-keeping. Did she even write anything down after her loss? Did she destroy the diary so her future children from another husband would never know all that she would grieve for the rest of her life? She emerges from the war somber and heartbroken, as did so many of that lost generation. The man she had loved was dead. The world she had known was gone. Ten million soldiers died during World War I. Another ten million were irreparably wounded inside and out.

Mr. Havens wrote to her. He had never stopped thinking of her throughout all these years. Might she reconsider his proposal?

I was always led to believe that their marriage was the last resort of an aging spinster no one had claimed. She'd been left on the shelf, the girl no one really wanted. Even her parents wanted to get rid of her, marry her off, send her away. My grandmother was always presented to me as a failure—at marriage, motherhood, life. Under no circumstance should I ever imagine that I was in any way like this woman. I must guard against it, always. But I didn't notice the obvious, which was that this handsome up-and-coming lawyer in New York City did not want any of the many alluring women surely available to him on the cusp of the Jazz Age. My dowdy gray grandmother had once been the woman this man could not forget.

And he was the only man left for her to wed. And marriage was the only profession for a woman of her class.

I don't think my mother ever read the diaries. They were strewn haphazardly through the trunk. Certainly she'd never mentioned them.

I made myself a cup of tea and looked outside at the sea of blue forget-me-nots that circled my house. All of them had grown from a single sprig I had taken from my mother's garden. Hers had come from a single plant she had dug up from her mother's garden. Nellie had brought the forget-me-not seeds with her from England. I went back to the diaries.

Nellie married my grandfather the day after he arrived in London—after not seeing him for four years, after only having known him less than a month even then, after becoming an entirely different person altogether than the young British maiden he'd rescued so daringly. She married a stranger. He married a stranger.

"I was raped on my wedding night," my grandmother once confessed to my mother. "We were both virgins and he didn't know what he was doing—it was terrifying and painful."

Two days after they were wed, she got on a boat with her husband and headed across the ocean to a new country and an entirely different way of life. She was no longer surrounded by a cozy coterie of cousins and familiar friends. Mr. Havens was a very sophisticated modern American man, arguing about art and politics over cocktails, playing bridge and chess, always up for a game of tennis, always ready to make a deal. He was not sure if they should have a dog in the city. He hated to get his hands dirty. He certainly did not want to talk about how there might be fairies in the back garden. Two weeks after their boat docked, Nelly wrote in her diary that "*I have explained to Mr. Havens that I am headed home. He seems to understand that this is not the right place for me.*"

She is elated on her trip back to England, spending hours on the deck watching the sun glint across the ocean, the whales breaching in the distance, the seagulls announcing that they are nearing land. Her parents are waiting for her on the docks. Her little bed in the bedroom with the pink rose wallpaper is waiting for her. The forget-me-nots are blooming in the back garden. But by the time she is back in her old house, it is clear to everyone that she is pregnant.

In the novel *Life After Life*, the British author Kate Atkinson imagines a single life lived a hundred different ways, each destiny unfurling from a choice here or an unexpected event there. There is the life my grandmother might have lived if her veterinarian had not died. There is the life she might have lived if she could have gone to school or had a career. There is the life she might have lived if she had not arrived home pregnant with my mother. Here is the life she was condemned to because women who got pregnant by their husbands did not get divorced.

She fell into a listless state of despair when she was told she would have to head back to America. There was no other choice. For a year, arrangements were discussed back and forth in letters. Eventually Mr. Havens arrived with his mother and his sister to bring her back, to claim his child, his wife, his property. He was making a lot of money as a lawyer, he told her. He had bought a big house out near the beach where they could throw huge boozy parties on the weekend. She didn't care. He had bought a big fast car to get to his great big house. She didn't care. He was going to hire lots of servants—cooks and housemaids and gardeners and chauffeurs—so she would never have to work a day in her life. She didn't care.

She barely wrote in her diary about the baby—not the child's birth, not her name, not her first words or steps.

*"In bed."*
*"In bed."*
*"In bed."*

Day follows day follows depressing day.

A year after my mother was born she noted for the first time, "*Helped Nurse give baby a bath today.*" Soon there was another baby, and she refused to get up out of bed. She refused to talk or eat. She didn't care about anything. One night when the big house was full of heated conversations about who was really the best artist or the best writer or the best tennis player, she walked down to the beach and decided that it was time for her to go home. She followed the stars, swimming out farther and farther into the ocean. She didn't care if she perished. But the currents carried her back to shore, and she didn't die—her parents did, both of them within months of each other, of heart failure. Then her husband left her for another woman, because it turned out you could get divorced in America after all. Only now she had no idea where she really belonged.

Was there ever a life for my grandmother in America? Was there ever a life where she made her way back home to England? She kept the little house she moved into after the divorce immaculate and spent hours with her flowers. She started a garden club to bring other women together and share seeds and lore. She became an advocate, in the 1930s, for easy access to birth control and abortion. She encouraged her daughter's passions for art, for literature, for men.

"Lie about your age," she urged when my mother, only seventeen, wanted to be a costume designer with the Federal Theatre Project.

"Tell them I'll move with you and be your chaperone," she said, when the Yale Drama School wasn't sure they could accept a woman into their graduate program.

"Please read this book before tonight," she told my mother, giving her a pamphlet on marital relations. "And make sure you get yourself a diaphragm."

But daughters so often do not understand the sorrows and tribulations of their mothers. My mother knew in her bones that her birth changed the course of her mother's life and she didn't know why. My mother never read her mother's diaries. She knew her mother had no one else in the world but her. She knew that her mother had always wanted another life. Was she too close to her mother—or not close enough? What if every one of our grandmothers had kept such a diary and we could bear witness to the day-to-day experience of their lives?

My mother did talk to the psychiatrists who treated my grandmother. Their confidential reports were also in the steamer trunk. "A chronic depressive with a neurotic attachment to both her mother and her daughter." "An upper middle class woman of middling intelligence and few passions or interests." "Subject rarely masturbates and does not exhibit healthy sexual maturity." "Uneducated with few intellectual inclinations." "Prognosis is not hopeful." "Recommended course of treatment: hydrotherapy and electric shock." In none of their extensive interviews did they ask her about how to make things grow even when you yourself were withering.

Throughout it all my grandmother faithfully kept her diaries. Wherever she was, whether at home or in an institution, she could note the weather each day. There were so many types of rain, so many kinds of clouds, so many different colors of the sky. Even silenced by her series of strokes, lying in a hospital bed, staring out the window, she still had the weather.

It took me three days to read all of the diaries. When I was done, I took myself out for a tromp through the woods. I stood up on the ridge beyond our backyard and looked back at my little house where I lived with my haiku poet. Not a veterinarian but a nature lover, not someone who would ever want a fast-paced life with a new car every year. We had fled the competitive materialism of New York City early in our marriage to make a home in the woods. A long time ago, before my mother was even conceived, I was already inside my grandmother's body and she had already bequeathed to me her dreams.

The original divine Trinity was not, as Christianity asserts, the Father, the Son, and the Holy Ghost but rather the Triple Goddess: the Maiden, the Mother, and the Crone. Our ancient ancestors identified these women with the changing phases of the moon—waxing, full, and dark—but they also intuited the profound connection between these three generations; they knew that these three bodies had once all been one body. They knew that the strength and intimacy of their clan were the shared dream of these three women. Women stayed together; it was the men who might leave one group and join another. But patriarchy is about dividing the world into pieces—about separating human beings from all other beings, heaven from Earth, mind from body, soul from life, and women from each other.

To imagine what our ancestral grandmothers have endured is to risk overwhelming ourselves with so many generations of trauma and horror—to feel resentful of all we must heal because of them, for them, for ourselves.

Only the dead do not need to be healed.

When I became a mother myself, I began to see with the eyes of the dead. At first, I felt so utterly alone. I had various books that told me what I should do, what milestones my child should be achieving, and when I should call the doctor. But my own mother was far away and in the middle of chemotherapy. My husband and I, sleepless and exhausted, were reeling between work and childcare, and my friends who were also parents had the same books, the same cultural expectations, and the same isolation and anxiety. I found myself with the baby at my breast in the middle of the night, longing for the grounded wisdom of old women who'd seen it all. There was what everyone—the books, the experts, the prevailing lore—told me I *should* do and there was what I longed to do. Where were these ancient grandmothers who could help me become a mother?

My own grandmothers were both long since dead, but I began to feel them guiding me in the quiet darkness, leading me back to my own intuitions. Molly, who had raised six children on no money, obviously helped me tap into my resourcefulness and showed me how to make ends meet.

"Go into your basement," I told Molly, "Open that jar of wishbones at last, grant us our wishes from near and from far."

Did she play a part when my husband unexpectedly sold a little book on haiku poetry for enough money to quit our city jobs, move to the mountains, and buy a house? I can't prove it, of course, but I can claim the wish she granted, the miracle she facilitated. Stingy in life, Molly became profligate with her blessings from the other side of the veil. I found myself calling on her, laughing with her, thanking her each and every day.

Calling on Nellie was harder, because in the beginning she felt like such a diffuse cloud of sorrow. But after my mother's death, after I read the diaries, the kids and I found an injured goose in the middle of the road that we nursed back to health with the help of a local wildlife rehabilitator. Soon we were nursing swans and ducks, baby possums and chipmunks. I called on Nellie and her veterinarian as I learned how to chelate a bird dying from heavy metal poisoning or help a stunned owl recover from shock. When my own child became sick, years later, I was used to turning to Nellie. I trusted her by then.

As I sent my prayers and blessings out to Nellie wherever she was and as I felt, not the burden of her mental illness, but the dreams of the young woman, I realized how much my own life owed to her—my love of daily walks through fields and mountains, my love of the natural world, my love of the weather in all of its unpredictability, even if I didn't write about it every day. With a start I realized something I'd never been told, never imagined: my grandmother had been a writer just like me.

I had modeled my life on her husband, the Rhodes scholar, winning academic awards and striving to be the best at all I did. But he never wrote anything. He just became a lawyer and made money. I modeled myself on my well-read father, devouring the books in his library, but he also never wrote anything either despite his poetic pretensions. No, it was my grandmother from whom I had received my desire to make sense of the world through words. She was my real predecessor. What if she had stayed in England, surrounded by that community of groundbreaking writers? What might her diaries have become if her passions had been encouraged by warm and gentle souls? Who knows what she might have done with her life? Another possibility, a whole other life—my own life—opened up in front of me.

Whatever they endured in any particular incarnation, those on the other side have been liberated from the miseries and shortcomings of a single incarnation. They have recovered the long story of their souls through deep time and the dreams they have held from one life to another. What once felt disappointing, impossible, and upsetting as the years slid by for a living person is suddenly possible again to the dead. We have more lives than we can imagine to make our dreams come true, to see our prayers answered. To see with the eyes of the dead is to know that our story is a long story with so many more twists and turns and returns than we can imagine. To see with the eyes of the dead is to know that the future stretches before us into eternity and there is all the time in the world for the magic of life itself.

My grandmother, dead, wasn't depressed anymore.

I wondered about the life she had been reborn into. Did she find her way back to England at last? Did she and her veterinarian reunite in new bodies and new lives with hearts that remembered each other? Maybe she was a veterinarian now, or maybe she was an animal or a tree with roots deep in the earth, the sun filling her leaves with green warmth. Maybe she was the brown wren that circled my head when I stepped outside on my front porch on star-filled summer nights.

More and more grandmothers from the other side began showing up to help as I raised my children. Some of them were distant relatives; others were neighbors and friends I'd known growing up. Some of them were pets—Fluffernutter, the mother of over sixty kittens. Some of them were trees—the hemlock next to the library whose branches held me in a secret world as I read and traveled in my imagination. Some of them were men who had cared for me as mothers, my friends asking me about my heart even as they succumbed to AIDS. Soon I was calling on all the dead I'd ever known—from the stranger who'd died in my friend's apartment building to the groundhog hit by a car to another stranger whose passing moved me for reasons I could not explain. I wanted the dead to help me, and I had a feeling that they could.

What if the fairies that my grandmother's childhood circle believed in were nothing but the forgotten souls of the dead? What if the magic they brought to the world was real—and available to all of us if we could begin collaborating with those on the other side? I began to realize that on the other side all the dead, whoever or whatever they were in life, remembered that they were mothers.

The only stories I was told about my grandmother growing up were about her depression and what a burden she was to everyone around her. I grew up on guard against any signs of mental instability, terrified by my own encounters with the unseen world. But what if I'd been told the story of the courageous nurse, the outdoorswoman, the devoted diarist? What if I had known who she really was, not just what she had endured but what she had dreamed? What if I had known that the waters all around me were not meant to drown me but to carry me where I needed to go?

The stories we tell about our grandmothers matter because they tell us who we are and who we might become. To heal our ancestors, we only need to tell bigger and wider stories about them—that will in turn let us tell bigger and wider stories about ourselves.

Do our stories condemn them, vilify them, or dismiss them? What if, instead, we gave our grandmothers back their dreams and their power? We can undo generational trauma only when we begin telling new stories about who our ancestors really were.

Once a student of mine recounted the tale of her grandmother who had fled her own father's violence and entered the convent, only to be raped by a priest and then married off to another abusive man when she became pregnant. My student had always felt oppressed by this horrific story, her grandmother's victimhood, and especially her eventual suicide. After the birth of her tenth child, this grandmother had thrown herself off the roof. "But I think that night she finally realized that she had wings. I see her walking up to the top of her apartment building and spreading her arms. She realizes that she has the power to fly away. I'm proud of her now, seeing her like that. I really am." My student, on the Zoom screen, began to weep. She knew her grandmother would always protect her, always help her fly. She wasn't just the granddaughter of a miserable victim anymore but of a woman who had reached for a life beyond pain.

Let us tell new stories about our grandmothers together. The grandmother who was a lifelong alcoholic knows how to help us get sober. The grandmother who wasn't educated can help us get into college. The grandmother who died young can help us claim our health and longevity. Once we know that the dead are real and the story of a soul is never over, then we can begin to find new ways to tell the histories of our ancestors that liberate us from their sorrows.

We do not undo the curses our grandmothers have carried by running away from them—but by embracing the totality of who they were. Each of these women is more than a diagnosis or a verdict. Let us together tell new stories about who our grandmothers were, who they might have been, and who they are becoming even now.

Jezebel, the whore of Babylon, the queen maligned for millennia, gave away the holy city to the pagan gods and became a symbol of the worst that women can become. But to reread her history in context is to discover a woman embracing religious tolerance and welcoming spiritual diversity into her community at the risk of her own life. When she is eventually condemned to death by priestly authorities, she adorns herself with jewels and henna and the trappings of royalty before she is fed to the dogs. She does this not because she is a brazen hussy but because she will not surrender her self-worth to small, vindictive men.

Eve is friends with the snake, who has long been the symbol of rebirth and renewal. She knows that even as her husband forgets the long story of his soul and embraces a life of toil and death, she will place her foot above the snake, touch its head lightly with her toes, give it a caress, to remember what can always be remembered by us all: life is not linear—it is circular, merciful, and generous. Life, like the demonized snake, always renews itself.

Jezebel, Eve, our traumatized grandmothers, our complicated mothers—we don't need to rescue them from their lives once they are dead. But we can tell new stories about these women that give them back their agency and help us remember our own power.

Whatever is in our hearts began in the bodies of our grandmothers. We can call out to them, summon them into our lives, and ask them to help us make the impossible possible, give us the miracles we need, and return to us the magic we had thought we'd lost. Our grandmothers are always as close as our own hearts.

# A Message from the Oldest of Grandmothers

Most of my names are forgotten. I have been called Tiamat, Anu, and the very Chaos of the Deep itself. I am all of your grandmothers and all of your mothers. Your soul first unfurled in my dark waters. I speak to you from the mysteries at the bottom of the ocean and the darkest depths of deepest time. I am the mother of all the mothers, but I, too, have a mother. I, too, was formed in the uncreated womb of the cosmos. I am the great mystery. You, too, are a mystery even to yourself.

Come, sit with me, and let me tell you the tale of how I died and did not die.

Once upon a time the bodies of your grandmothers did not frighten your people. You carved images of them from bone and stone and wood—all of matter, all that was, was the body of these women, the bodies that birthed your mothers and the body of the Earth that took you back at the end of your life. You looked at the drooping breasts and sagging bellies of these grandmothers and knew that you were home, that you belonged, that you were loved. You held these images of your naked grandmothers in your hands and felt them holding you. The whole Earth held you. I held the Earth; I held your grandmothers; and I held you.

When did you first start to fear your grandmothers? Why did you reject them and push them away? How did it possibly happen that you forgot how much they love you, how much I have always loved you?

Oh, the grandmothers all overlooked so much in the beginning. Should we have worried when you began to plant the same seeds in the same places over and over again? But so many of our creatures garden for us—digging, sowing, carrying, pollinating. You still followed the rhythms of the seasons and the herds, trusting us to feed you and care for you. You still walked on the earth and knew it was our body that bore you up, guided you, and received you at the end. You still trusted when you died that you would always return, that there was nowhere that you could go that we would not embrace you.

So, no, we didn't worry, and then we drifted off, as grandmothers do, in and out of our dreams, back and forth between worlds . . . for a year, another year, an age. We woke one day and found that you had begun to plant more grains, and now that was all you wanted to eat. You wanted to eat these grains every day, and you wanted to eat them all year long. You began to mistrust what we offered to you and to fear the times when we asked that you live lean and remember how to die. You couldn't get enough wheat and barley, rice and corn. We tried to entice you with delectables. Those years our trees gave more nuts than ever; the flocks grew, and there were eggs in every nest; the seas teemed with fish. But you were drunk on grain.

Later on you will pretend it was bread you wanted, but it was really wine and beer in the beginning. Intoxication fuddled you. In truth it was only a few of you. We do not condemn you all. But what trouble those few made as they reeled about imagining themselves kings and rulers and gods.

"This is *my* land," slurred one of our grandsons. "This is *my* grain. This is *my* beer. This is *my* woman. These are *my* children. These are *my* slaves to grow *my* grain. This is *my* army to make my women and my children and my slaves behave."

The grandmothers went to the old men and poured forth our worries. "They've forgotten who they are and to whom they belong. They are drunk all day, not just on beer but most of all on their own power. They are forgetting how to belong and only wanting to acquire and to control."

"A bad batch," muttered Apsu, one of the grandfathers. He'd been humming one of the songs to the birds as his own soul got ready to fly away. "Get rid of them. A flood maybe? A volcano, a meteor. Time to start over, oh yes time to start over . . ." He dozed off and began to snore.

"No!" we gasped, horrified. After all, they were our grandchildren—and it was so much work starting the world all over again, after the fires or the waters or the dying times.

But even the grandmothers make mistakes. We are artists, and all artists make mistakes.

That is what it means to make things.

That very night one of our grandsons snuck through the reeds to where we were sleeping on the beach. The surf rolled in and out as Apsu slept beside me. The sky was dark and filled with stars. The ocean was dark. The reflection of the moon washed across the surface of the deep. The boy, his breath stale and rancid, cut the throat of his grandfather and left him beside me to die. "Don't you ever plan our demise again," he hissed before slinking off into the shadows.

My fury was wild. I sent locusts to decimate their fields. I sent plagues to destroy their herds. Some of them, most of you, tried to run back into the wilderness, but our grandsons hunted these people down like the beasts they no longer thought they were. They would not change their ways. They became drunker on their power, settling into the land, settling into their violence, settling into their misery and mistakes. They despised their grandmothers.

"Away with you!" they shouted. "Cover your nakedness! Your withered teats disgust us. You don't make anything. You don't give us children anymore. You are useless, barren scolds."

They feared the grandmothers even as they cursed them and me. They feared my waters, which could rise and drown them. They feared the unpredictability of my winds. They feared all that I remembered and all that I could see before them. They feared the darkness of my body and the mystery of my ways.

Marduk came for me at last with his sword. He split me like a shellfish into pieces, pulling out my guts and hurling them onto the dirt. He cut off my breasts. "I will feed my people. Not you!" His spittle landed on my cheeks wet with tears that became a river of sorrow. He lifted his blade and plunged it into my heart. "You are a monster," he hissed, "and you deserve to die."

Marduk thought he was so clever. He began leveling the forests. He changed the courses of the rivers. He planted more and more grain and filled his storehouses with his bounty. When his fields were exhausted, he cursed me and went in search of other lands to rape and mine and conquer. "That woman made a mess of everything," he explained to his subjects. "We will get the world organized again. Let us divide the light from the dark, the good from the bad, the men who are good and light from the women who are bad and dark. I am giving to you a day of rest but please do not remember that once upon a time when the grandmothers held you there was no work, there was only life. Oh, those old crones, those old hags, those old biddies. It's their fault, you know, that you are going to die."

He told a story about how a woman was the cause of all their problems.

The women he had beaten, the slaves he had whipped, the soldiers he had traumatized cowered in terror. His boot was on their backs.

"One last thing," he said. "Thou shalt have no other gods but me."

Most of you wanted to run away and find your lost grandmothers, so the sons of Marduk had to make codes and laws to get civilization right. But they could never get it just right because it has always been wrong. They made promises and built prisons. Once you had culture without violence. You sang with the birds, danced with the trees, made art, and told stories of your kin. The sons of Marduk took away your tales and gave you scriptures etched on stones.

"These are the lineages of the men that matter. These are the battles we have waged and won. This is why we men are so important," they explained to those they had silenced into submission.

The bodies of your grandmothers, the bodies of this earth, have been divided by roads and railways and express lanes. They have been mined and plundered and raped. They have been poisoned and clear-cut. Each new violation is a sword in our hearts.

But the sons of Marduk could not silence the beating of *my* heart.

Stand at the shore and listen to the waves and hear the heart of the ocean. Stand on the mountain and listen to the wind and hear the heart of the world. Hear me, the grandmother of your grandmothers, in the steady whir of the katydids, the rush of the water down the stream, the mournful cry of the owl. Press your body close to the earth and you will feel my heart beating with yours. In their dreams, your most devout artists will envision the Mother with a sword in her heart and paint her for all to see. They will call her Maria Dolorosa, Our Lady of Sorrows, and say that she is weeping for her son nailed to a cross. But I do not weep for one child. I weep for all my children. I weep for life itself.

Come, my children. Your grandmothers are still here. I am still here. Soon all of this—the roads and towers and machines—will be no more than a dream that your people can barely remember. Our laps are wide; our arms are many; our hearts are mighty. All this time we've been here making the soup, watching you through the night, keeping an eye out for the little ones, lending a hand here and there. Go sit with one of your grandmothers—her eyes are watery, her back hunched, and her hands gnarled. Touch one of her hands and ask her for her story. It is time to put away the books of men and remember the stories of our grandmothers.

We are ready to lead you back to the old mysteries and the old ways. We are ready to help you remember how to be wild. We are here to answer your prayers—but now it is time for you to remember what you are really praying for.

## Chapter Five

# OUT OF THE FIRES

Over many years I worked on a book about my experiences connecting with those on the other side of the veil. I wanted to share what I had discovered about collaborating with the ancestors, about how generous and helpful they were, even those who had been difficult when they were alive. It had become a daily habit for me to reach out to the dead—to my parents, to relatives, to friends, to teachers, even to seeming strangers who showed up with gifts and guidance. Still, I was often surprised by how real the departed were and eager to be recognized for their presence in my life.

A month before the publication of my book *Take Back the Magic*, I broke out in a full-body rash. Red welts oozed between my toes, along the underside of my arms, between my fingers, all over my belly and my legs, around my eyes, and in the most private parts of me. I looked like I had been dipped in hot oil or a chemical bath or rescued just moments before some blazing fire consumed my entire body. I was blistered and suppurating. It was just awful.

I thought it was probably poison ivy, to which I am very allergic. I'm careful about gardening or even walking through fields carelessly, but sometimes one of the cats will rub against the vines and then rub up against me. When I first began itching, I grabbed the medicated scrub cream I use for exposures, showered, and assumed that in a day or two with careful tending I'd be better because this had happened a hundred times before. But the rash got worse. It spread; it oozed; it was angry. I couldn't sleep; I couldn't think. I was miserable, not to mention we were supposed to head out on our yearly trip to Cape Cod at the end of the week.

Clark wanted me to go to the emergency room. "It's all over your eyelids," he noted, truly concerned.

"They'll just want to put me on steroids again," I said. The last time I'd gotten poison ivy on my face I'd taken prednisone and ended up with an acute case of pancreatitis, which it turns out is one of its side effects. I didn't want to go near those drugs again. "Anyway," I added, "I know it looks awful, and it feels awful, but I don't think the rash is life-threatening."

Instead, I went over for a consultation with the dead at my ancestor altar, or rather the wall of ancestors that was becoming the room of the ancestors around my dining room table ever cluttered with more memento mori. I had photos of grandparents and great-grandparents and ancient aunts in stiff corsets, faded daguerreotypes of Clark's stern Arkansas kin, funeral cards for friends and neighbors, pictures of pets, small statues of various saints and healing deities, and feathers and fossils of prehistoric sea creatures I had found on the local mountain.

I did not think of my ancestors as a lineage of names to which I was connected biologically but rather an entangled root system of beings who were the very ground from which I grew. All the dead who had ever been were our dead, were my dead, were there for me to call upon when I needed help.

I lit a candle; spritzed a little bit of my mother's favorite perfume, L'Air du Temps by Nina Ricci; poured a dram of the good bourbon into an offering bowl; and waited for inspiration. Who was going to help me get rid of this wretched rash?

My first thought when it came to anything medical was, of course, to call upon my father the doctor. After all, the book I was about to publish was ostensibly about our journey toward healing after he was gone. But the truth was that he hadn't really wanted to be a doctor, despite how talented he was at medicine. He'd wanted to be a writer but didn't feel, as the eldest son of immigrants, that it was a financially responsible path. Lately, I'd found him particularly helpful when I asked for his support making a living as an artist—selling my book for instance, earning royalties on another, getting paid to talk about my work. Every time some unexpected financial blessing arrived around my writing, I honored my father by memorizing one of his favorite poems, visiting his grave, or sharing publicly how yet again he was taking care of me from the other side.

I tried not to scratch and went through a list of all of the doctors I'd known at my dad's hospital. I thought about all of the nurses I used to hang out with at the ER while I waited for him. No one felt quite right for this problem for reasons I couldn't explain. Maybe it was because I couldn't think of a single dermatologist who'd been buddies with my father . . . or something.

Clark, passing through the room, joked, "Are you looking for an ancestor to help who was exiled to a leper colony?"

"Stop!" I shouted.

I scanned the shelves looking at the photos. Maybe he was right. Was there anyone among my kith and kin who'd struggled with skin problems? Often when people have experienced defeats or failures in life, they are supercharged to help with those very same issues once they have the perspective of the long story. The frustrated writer can help us get our book done. The great-grandmother with incurable eczema might now know how to make our rash vanish. Who was the patron saint of poison ivy?

For no reason that I could discern I thought of an ancestral grandmother. I certainly didn't have a photo of this woman from the seventeenth century. I didn't even know her name. But I knew that my mother's father's family was descended, male Havens by male Havens, from a man named William Havens who had arrived in Boston in 1640 and, fed up with the Puritans, had headed down to what would become Rhode Island with the religiously tolerant Roger Williams. It was his wife, however, that suddenly popped into my head. She had had thirteen children, which was why, whenever I met someone with the surname Havens, there was a great likelihood we were related if we went back far enough. Other than that, I hadn't really thought about her before. I mean, go back eight generations and we all have well over a thousand grandparents to get to know.

But in that moment I had a vision of a mother with thirteen children, raising her family in an unfamiliar ecosystem and having to manage those thirteen children getting into poison ivy all summer long. Surely she had some long-lost remedies that might serve her distant descendant. Surely by the thirteenth kid she knew some way to stop the scratching. Needless to say, she didn't have steroids or Benadryl cream at her disposal.

In order to formally ask for her help, I felt like I should at least know her name. I hopped online, grateful for the distraction of research, and began hunting through the voluminous Havens genealogy available on various blogs. I don't actually spend much time on ancestry sites, preferring to welcome whatever souls from the other side show up. There are so many after all, but Mrs. William Havens had decided to step to the forefront of my mind. I quickly discovered that while she was sometimes called Denise or Denis, she was officially known in the earliest records as Dionyse.

As the old fairy tales remind us, names hold a certain kind of magic. To know a name is to know who someone really is. Sometimes these names are spells in and of themselves.

The children of Dionyse all had typical early New England names—Martha, Elizabeth, Rebecca, and Ruth. Good biblical names. Familiar Puritan-era names. But Dionyse, as more research confirmed, derived from Dionysus, the ancient Greek god of revelry and rebellion. My itchy red skin was now prickling with a thousand goose bumps. My daughter had just published a book of her own—about Dionysus. More specifically, her collection of essays was about how men need other stories and other gods to help them recover from the violence of patriarchy. Her book was called *The Flowering Wand* in tribute to the generative *thyrsus* or wand that Dionysus employs instead of the destructive sword.

My ancient ten times great-great-grandmother was, coincidentally, named for an ancient Greek god that my daughter was writing about all the time.

The dead see more and know more than we do. They see how the puzzle pieces fit together. They can see the big picture on the front of the puzzle box. Most of what we experience is a mystery to us. We feel two unexpected puzzle pieces from all those strewn across the table clicking into place but are not necessarily sure what has just happened. I felt something much bigger than I understood beginning to unfold.

But in the meantime, I needed to do something about my rash. I headed out to the local big-box pharmacy with its aisles of ointments and creams in the hopes that inspiration or guidance might arrive from Dionyse. I found myself standing in front of the usual assortment of remedies I'd already tried feeling more than a little hopeless. I felt like clawing off my skin.

"Have you tried Domeboro?" asked a nondescript woman standing beside me. Middle-aged, in relaxed brown slacks. Brown hair.

"What's that?" I asked.

"It's an astringent scrub they use in a lot of hospitals when people get poison ivy as badly as you have it."

"I tried a scrub . . ." I began.

"Domeboro is the secret weapon," she interrupted. She grabbed a box from the bottom shelf. "Really. I'm a nurse. I swear by it. That and witch hazel will calm everything down."

"Okay!" I said, grateful for at least something new to try. "It really works?"

"It really works," she said. "You look miserable."

"Thanks, yeah, I am. Thank you again. Excuse me, what's your name? Are you local?"

"I live across the river, but I'm here visiting a friend. My name's Denise."

Denise. Denis. Dionyse.

"Thank you," I gulped, my mouth dry. But the woman was already gone.

At home I scrubbed with my new scratchy powder and drenched myself in witch hazel, which I figured was probably available a couple of centuries ago too. I instantly felt better and was able to finish the packing for our family vacation and get a good night's sleep at last. Just before I drifted off, I promised Dionyse that I would find out where she was buried and one day visit her grave, even though I had the nagging feeling that there was something I was missing.

Still, I woke up confident that I was all better, gave myself another treatment, and we all piled into the car for the long drive to my homelands. The closer we got to the ocean, the more my soul began to sing. I love the smell of salt in the air, the scrub pines growing bent and twisted in the sandy soil, the marsh grasses, the funk of low tide, the vastness of the sky stretching in all directions.

As I was growing up in New England, the Puritans felt like a ubiquitous presence. Every November our grade school class or our Girl Scout troop visited Plimoth Plantation to learn about early colonial life. My high school boyfriend lived in a house his family had built and lived in since the seventeenth century. When we read *The Crucible* in English class, the surnames were familiar, not just on gravestones but among my classmates. The traditional foods of Thanksgiving—the cranberries and the corn and the pumpkins—grew all around us. In winter we skated across the flooded cranberry bogs leaving lines of red, like blood seeping from beneath the skin of the frozen land.

I often felt anxious growing up. Much of that had to do with the volatility of my parents' marriage, and some of it with the existential terrors of the Cold War that permeated life in those days, but I also traced my feelings of threat and danger to a movie I'd watched with a babysitter as a little girl. She'd made popcorn and sat us down in front of the television on a Sunday afternoon to watch *Crowhaven Farm*. It is a film about a woman, played by Hope Lange, who has just moved to an old clapboard house in a coastal Massachusetts village and is paranoid that her neighbors are out to get her. She is certain that beneath their preppy politeness, masked by their pressed khakis and polo shirts, they are actually reincarnated Puritan witch-hunters come to lead her to the gallows yet again. In one terrifying scene, her husband, who has not believed her, discovers them pressing her beneath giant stones to see if she will confess. I sat there mesmerized and horrified, convinced that what I was watching was the absolute truth.

Reasonable men, people convinced of their righteousness and goodness, could do terrible things. I already knew this was true even as a little girl. I knew that the churchgoing father of a friend was a monster to her behind closed doors. I knew that the best and the brightest could coldly calculate the worst and the stupidest—from the war in Vietnam to the making of the atomic bomb. I had suspected that beneath the pretty window boxes filled with geraniums, underneath the blossoming hydrangeas, moldering somewhere beneath layers of seaweed and sand, the land itself remembered the atrocities of the European conquerors.

As a teenager *The Crucible* made me furious. All blame for the Salem witch trials was placed on the heads of hysterical girls and a seductive teen temptress—as usual. Yes, it was a metaphor for the McCarthy hearings, but more insidiously it told young female readers that they better behave, not get too emotional or out of control, or innocent people just might die. It wasn't the men who held all the power who were the problem; it was the unruly girls. Never once did we discuss the fact that without the good men of Harvard going up to Salem and setting up their courts and parsing their legal documents, no one would ever have been tried or hanged. The gallows would never have been built. Never once did we discuss the misogyny of the man who had written the play. Never once did we explore just how prevalent witch accusations were in the colonial world and just how many women were tried and condemned and murdered throughout the original thirteen colonies. What happened in Salem was treated as a onetime aberration and not something that was happening everywhere in the colonial world.

By the time we reached our rental house at the very tip of Cape Cod, I was more inflamed than I had ever been. I was on the edge of screaming. Not only did it now seem like the treatment wasn't working; it might just have made everything worse.

"Placebo effect the first few times," suggested Clark. "I'm not sure that new stuff is helping after all."

"It's the air," said Sophie. "Did you know that the ocean air diffuses microtoxins? People used to go to the beach to get better, and now it makes them sicker. Not to mention we're downwind of the Pilgrim nuclear plant."

"How are you feeling?" asked Jonah. "Maybe a dip in the ocean and some time in the sun will help."

We changed into our suits and headed out to the beach just in time to watch the sunset. The wild roses in the dunes were in bloom. The steady crash of the waves against the shore soothed my nerves, and I walked down to the water for a bracing plunge. My kids often joke that I spent more time in the water when they were kids than they did, that I must have been a seal in a past life. I always feel like I'm home when I'm immersed in the ocean. The cold Atlantic soothed my burning skin, and I stood there, my feet grazing the pebbles in the sand, the currents lapping me back and forth now closer to land, now farther away.

I had written a book about the power of talking to the dead, and I knew, from copious research over the years, that the crime women were most often accused of during the Burning Times was not midwifery or herbalism or even hysteria or mental illness, as is often assumed, but the everyday practice of consulting with loved ones on the other side. A woman might whisper a prayer to her grandmother or an old aunt and find herself accused. A mother might call on a guardian grandfather and find herself condemned. A girl might make a poppet that reminded her of a long-gone auntie and allowed her to feel protected by her. But the men in charge didn't want women to listen to the dead as they had done for millennia; they wanted them to obey the living in power.

Drifting in the shallows in the dusk as the first stars began to appear, I felt Dionyse close. She had something to tell me about those times. I had read what books I could find, and it was remarkable how little research had been done, town to town, about what really happened in that terrifying period that spanned centuries and continents. There was no single database to track just how many people had died in the American colonies, how many people had been accused and what the generational effects had been on the survivors. The explanations for the violence—a superstitious reaction to illness or cataclysm, acquisitive greed for land and property—always seemed to miss something essential about what it means when a people, a culture, wants to kill, terrify, or silence all its women. What was it like to be a woman during those times? I was on fire, and Dionyse would help me put the fire out—if only I could listen to what she was really saying.

What had changed most since I had begun claiming my work with the dead was that I trusted my intuition about their guidance.

After we'd all had outdoor showers, eaten our annual batch of fried clams, and finally headed to bed, I opened my computer and set out to find out what I could about Dionyse. In any case, there was no way I was going to sleep with my body feeling so miserable.

We know so little about so many of our ancestors, especially the women. Sometimes all we have is a single anecdote or even a single fact: She died in childbirth. Her child died young. Her husband was famous, but she was not. Sometimes what we know feels like we don't want to know it: She was the crazy one. She was a bitch. A single word becomes an epitaph and a legacy passed down across the generations. How do we give our ancestors back their stories, their power, and their lived reality?

It's not enough to know birth and death dates and places of origin. We want to know who they were. We want to know, when we collaborate with them, how they can help us. What are their gifts? What wisdom did their lives bring forth from within them? How do their failings and their sorrows become their superpowers? How might a single fact bloom into a real person that we can call upon in our hour of need?

We have to allow ourselves to activate our imaginations and trust our intuitions.

Dionyse came to Boston in 1640. She was from Sheffield, Yorkshire, and she was sixteen years old. She journeyed by herself without her parents, a brother or sister, or any other relatives. What compels a young woman to leave her home behind and take a dangerous journey across an ocean to an unknown wilderness? Certainly, she must have had courage, but she may also have been compelled by desperation. I could imagine all kinds of scenarios—an unwelcome suitor, an abusive family member, the death of a beloved, or simply, as her name implies, a rebellious spirit. On a hunch, however, I began exploring how prevalent the witch hunts were in her part of England in the 1600s.

All around her when she was growing up, women were being accused, tried, and hung. Just before she was born, ten people were murdered for witchcraft at Pendle Hill, less than a day's journey from her home. The old ways of being and knowing as women were under attack from both sides of the religious wars. Kill ten women and ten thousand women will get the message. It was no longer safe to practice the folk traditions of ages past. Most of all it was no longer safe to communicate with plants and animals and ancestors.

But Dionyse fled the frying pan and ended up in the fire and brimstone of the inflexible Puritans. Within a year she had left Boston and joined Anne Hutchinson down in Rhode Island. Hutchinson was a famous dissenter, an early advocate for women's rights, and an avowed troublemaker. My daughter Sophie had written about how Dionysus was often accused of making women go wild—but that was only the perspective of men who were trying to control the women. From the women's point of view—women confined to their households, subjugated by their husbands, forced into narrow gender roles—Dionysus brought them into the wilderness to free them of civilization's constraints, which was why he was often also called Liber. He was their liberator.

Dionyse met William Havens in Rhode Island and married him. It's hard to find out much information about them after their marriage because they didn't join any church or meetinghouse, not even the peace-loving Quakers. They lived out in the marshlands close to the ocean eking out a living from the fields and bringing thirteen children into the world. In his will William left everything to Dionyse, with the faith that she would continue to take care of their kin.

I like to think of them all around the fire at night, the wind whistling outside, and wonder what stories from the old country Dionyse told to her sons and daughters—and what stories she didn't tell. Soon after her first child was born, the witch trials began in the "new world." In 1649 a flu epidemic decimated Hartford, Connecticut. One young mother, Alyse Young, successfully nursed her daughter through the illness. When her daughter survived while the local pastor's didn't, Alyse was condemned and hung as a witch. Her husband did not intercede on her behalf, and her own daughter would carry the stain of her mother's murder, ever after accused of witchcraft herself. More trials and more murders followed, although there is no comprehensive list of all the people accused of witchcraft in America. The famous Salem witch trials, often presented as an aberration, a moment of madness, were simply the culmination of a program determined to eradicate other ways of being and knowing in the world. The Indigenous peoples were subjected to the worst genocide in human history; innumerable plants and animals were hunted to extinction; the worst system of slavery ever known was established and codified; and women were cut off from the empowering magic of their ancestors. No mumbo jumbo spiritual nonsense for them, only iron-willed fortitude and self-reliance.

What did Dionyse transmit to her seven daughters? Legions of well-behaved WASP women, tasteful strings of pearls around their necks, would trace their heritage back to Dionyse, but I can't help but think that my own wild mother was her true descendant. Maybe she was even Dionyse returned. People didn't used to worry so much about delineating ancestries when every great-grandmother was reborn as a grandchild.

There is a popular meme on social media that says, "We are the daughters of the women you could not burn." But there is deeper, older, wilder truth. We *are* the women you burned. We are the women who were tortured and raped, crushed and condemned, hung, drowned, and lashed to the stake. We are the women you tried to silence. And we are back. We always come back. Everyone comes back.

We can feel oppressed when we try to take in the enormous history of violence against women. We can feel weighted down by their miseries, their victimhood, their oppressions. But those women are dead, and no one needs to be rescued from death. Instead they are waiting for us to call upon them for help as we liberate *ourselves* from these genealogies of trauma. These women have known the worst horrors of patriarchy, and they know how to heal us and keep us safe.

My skin was on fire. My heart was on fire. I felt a holy rage burning within me. In the lead-up to my book's publication a number of friends had dropped away out of fear or jealousy. I knew that women had a hard time standing together, given our history, but it still felt terrible. To reclaim these lost conversations with the other side was to dredge up soul memories of such violence. But with Dionyse's help I could embrace my own rebellion and give voice to what we both knew.

"You look worse than ever," said Clark, coming into the living room bleary-eyed. "Have you been up all night?"

"I have," I said. "But now I'm ready to really heal."

Inspiration had struck, and I knew what to do about the inflammation coursing through my body. I needed an old folk remedy, and Dionyse had just let me know, with a passing thought, what it might be. "Go to the supermarket and get me a lot, I mean a lot, of plain yogurt, organic if they have it. This isn't poison ivy, or maybe it started that way, but now it's some kind of pernicious fungus. I need probiotics."

"You want me to get you some?"

"Yogurt will do," I said with confidence.

When Clark got back, I poured tubs of yogurt into the bath and marinated in it. When I got out, my skin was remarkably better. A few more baths and I was fully healed.

My gratitude to Dionyse was profound. I brought home a shell from the beach to represent her on my ancestor altar, but I found myself wondering if I should not commission from some artist friend a painting of an early colonial woman out on the marshlands, wondering about her past, sending her prayers into the future. I didn't need to bother.

The Sunday we got back from vacation Clark and I went to wander around the local flea market, and there, by one of the vendors, was a strange, large, framed photograph of a woman. Given the wavy quality of the glass, it seemed to have been made early in the last century. I asked the vendor where it had come from, and she shrugged. She'd picked it up at another flea market somewhere in Massachusetts. The photo showed a woman wearing a colonial costume—the cap, the cape, the familiar skirts. She is standing in the marshlands on a path that leads to the ocean, deep in thought.

I knew it was Dionyse.

I bought her for twenty dollars and brought her home and hung her, not in the dining room with all the other ancestors, but behind me in my office where I work and write about what was once forbidden.

I know she will always have my back.

# A Message from an Old Mother

You would think by now I would not be surprised by what good men can do in the name of empire and justice. Over so many lifetimes I have seen them inscribe their codes and laws, hold their courts and call their witnesses, announce their verdicts and prepare the pyres. I have seen how much they enjoy the interrogations and the torture. I have watched them cloak their violence in the authority of order and enlightenment for so long now. I have watched so many of our daughters, our sisters, our mothers, and our friends burn in the fires lit by reasonable men. My own daughter was burned alive by such men.

Let me tell you about my girl who listened to the voices of her ancestors and danced with them under the beech tree.

In those days we still had the old stories and followed the old ways. A bard might come in the winter and tell us the tales of that old shape-shifter Merlin and his prophecies, of the Lady who always came back to the lovers of the land, who would be called Jehanne, who would be born in an oak wood, who had always been our mother, our mother always come back. An old seer, weathered and worn, might ride into our village and over a crust of bread whisper to us that the Mother was returning to heal the world. "Her mother called her Jehanne," they'd say, "and her father called her D'arc."

Jehanne who was the ark, the holy covenant, the lost grail we'd all been seeking for so long to liberate us from the oppressions of pious priests. I knew it when I heard the bells ringing on the night that she was born.

No one read the Bible in those days. No one could even read, certainly not me or my daughter, not even the country priest. Ask someone in the country who Jesus was, and they might know or they might not. We laughed when we heard an old man, questioned by the authorities, say "Jesus? I know that fellow . . . he hangs upside down on his tree in the spring so his blood can renew the world." Oh, we laughed behind our hands. Because the old man still knew what mattered—the tree at the heart of the world, the blood that renews the land, the stories of his grandmothers. That old man knew that when a little girl was born to the sound of ringing bells in an oak wood she was the one the visionaries had foretold. He still listened, as we all did, to the songs of the birds, the whispers of the trees, the messages of the weather. The land was still our scripture. The earth was still our law.

Her father and I tried to stop her because we knew what was coming. But Jehanne rode into battle and performed wonders. All the king's men could not figure out how to put their kingdom back together again—but my daughter, who'd never even ridden a horse before, pulled the lost sword from the stone altar, triumphed over their enemies, crowned their prince, and won the hearts of the people who brought her their children to bless and their babes to bring back to life. But none of that was her real work; none of that was what she had come to do; none of that was even the miracle.

My pious girl's real battle was with the Church.

She was captured, betrayed, imprisoned, and brought before a tribunal of learned scholars, each one ready to parse her words and condemn her soul to hellfire. They knew already the outcome of their trial, but appearances mattered to them. They must seem reasonable, conclusive, and fair. No matter that they showed her the pincers and the rack. No matter that each night she was wrapped in chains and raped. No matter that they were already collecting the wood for her pyre.

Still, they were fools, as such men always are, and they wrote down everything she said. They wanted to inscribe their own greatness for history as they vanquished the witch, the heretic, the nineteen-year-old girl the people were whispering was really the queen of heaven and earth. They wanted to vanquish the whispers and the legends under an edifice of legality and paperwork. But the scribes didn't just write down their questions. They also recorded the Maid's wise and witty answers for posterity. My illiterate girl defeated, again and again, the most educated men of Christendom.

Eventually they burned my daughter alive. You think I did not feel each flame touch her skin? That I did not feel her lungs scorch and burn, that as far away as I seemed to be I did not hear her cries? But they could not burn her heart. One of those men reached into the embers, searing his hands, grabbed it still beating, and hurled it into the river, not even realizing he was giving her immaculate heart back to the earth itself.

Perhaps because they knew that they had lost, they amplified their efforts to silence our voices, the voices of their mothers and grandmothers. Most of all they wanted to silence the earth beating in rhythm with Jehanne's wild heart. They wanted to silence and terrify their wives and daughters. Their pronouncements became louder, their arguments more nuanced and complex. They invented a machine that would give birth to a thousand machines to impose their reality upon the world. Once they had inscribed their commandments onto stone, but now they cut down whole forests to print their laws on paper and distribute them throughout the kingdom. Less than ten years after Jehanne's murder, they began printing the Bible and demanding that men know how to read it. Thou shalt not suffer a witch to live. To ensure the truth of this they wrote another book, *The Malleus Maleficarum*, The Hammer of the Witches, justifying the terror and violence they were ready to unleash upon the world.

How many women were tortured and murdered? We did not keep accounting books—we wept and raged. In some villages not a single woman was left alive after the inquisitors had left. Daughters were encouraged to betray their mothers, mothers their daughters, neighbors and friends their sisters. The accused were subjected to elaborate tortures, pornographic tortures, until they confessed. They had felt the stirrings of sexual desire, so they must have been seduced by the devil. They didn't want to sleep with their husband, their lord, their priest, the man who held power over them, so they must be possessed. They dreamed they could fly, so they were demonic. They saw the future. They knew which plants healed. They left milk out for the kittens and the fairies, and they were suspect. They made poppets to hold their petitions to their ancestors. They whispered prayers to their mothers and grandmothers on the other side and were confirmed as witches. More than anything it was seeking solace and guidance from the dead that got them accused and condemned.

Thou shalt have no other gods but me.

Just as Tiamat's body had been split in two, so were women divided from each other—indoctrinated into fear and silence. Kill all the women in a single village, and the women for hundreds of miles around will know what is possible. They will hold that memory in their bones for hundreds of years. No wonder they will vilify each other for any behavior that might attract the wrong kind of attention. Don't get yourself noticed or we all might find ourselves swinging from the gallows. Don't dress like that. Don't speak like that. Don't do that. Nice girls don't.

Mothers feared for their daughters, and daughters feared their mothers as they became older and less fearful. After centuries of terror women learned to ally themselves with men for protection, instead of other women.

Lifetime upon lifetime I stood inside the fires with my mothers, my sisters, and my daughters.

The lie that these men will impose on their own history is that all of these events belonged to a distant superstitious past, a dark age when people would believe anything and knew nothing. The truth is that the worst horrors erupted in those places with the most educated of scholars in the very times when philosophy and the sciences were first emerging. There were more atrocities in the learned cities of Germany, of Scotland, of England, and of the Americas than in those places that still clung to the old ways and the old stories. These men were sure the entire world could be divided into pieces, categorized, organized into hierarchies of meaning, analyzed, and understood. There was no mystery that could withstand the minds of great men of learning. The whole world could be conquered, colonized, documented, mined, plowed, known, and owned. The Age of the Enlightenment, the whole modern world, was built on a foundation of horrors. The wholesale terror against women is not a side effect of "progress" but the basis of it.

It never really ended.

If the attacks against white women subsided, they only increased against Indigenous women, enslaved women, and any woman on the margins of society and colonial power. Not to mention the virgin forests that were leveled, the rivers that were dammed, the fields that were irradiated by chemicals and bombs. We feel in our bodies each of those fires, each of those violations, each of those atrocities.

Violence against one woman, or a small group of women, in the aftermath of the official witch craze became an effective means of forcing all other women into conformity and obedience. Our legacy from all of those mothers and daughters burned, hung, drowned, mutilated, and buried alive is an almost never acknowledged soul-silencing terror handed down from one woman to another.

You must know that almost none of these women would have called themselves witches. I did not call myself a witch. I was a good wife and a mother. My daughter did not call herself a witch. She was a daughter, a maid, a pious lady. Those women that they burned were housewives and church ladies and spinsters and crones and maidens and good girls and bad girls. They were simply women whose only crime was their wombs. Men wanted to own the land and control the means of production.

Yet I tell you, as the mother of Jehanne, as the mother of these daughters, that they are done with being victims. They do not need to be rescued; they need to be remembered. They know the lost truth that we all return no matter what is done to us. This is the wisdom the men of empire most wanted to suppress and silence: the dead don't stay dead. As Jehanne's body turned to ash, a dove emerged from the flames—her soul set free and ready to return to another body and lead another army.

But this time her army is the Earth itself and all the souls that have suffered under the horrors of civilization.

Let us call on our ancestors who endured these atrocities to give us the courage we need to stand together with my daughter. They will empower us to recover their lost arts. With their help we will begin to trust our dreams and reveries again. They will help us recover our intuition and imagination. We will remember how to listen to our voices, receive their guidance, and collaborate with the unseen world.

Let us say the names of all those who died in the times of terror. Let us summon these souls to our cause. Who better to help us set the world right than those who were murdered to make it wrong?

## Chapter Six

# ARE YOU MY MOTHER?

"I was forty-two when my mother was born," I announced to my therapist the first time we met.

He paused, waiting for me to hear my mistake, my classic Freudian slip—which I did almost instantly. I laughed ruefully. "She has always expected me to be *her* mother. Ever since I was born."

I saw my first counselor in college when I felt existentially lost about my purpose in life, and he helped me to understand that my mother was a narcissist and that I made too many of my choices in a useless attempt to please her. I saw my next therapist when I got cold feet before marrying a man I'd only been dating for a few months. This therapist, also a man, helped me to see that marriage was the best way to extract myself from my mother's gravitational force. At the time I was living an hour from my mother, teaching drama, and we'd begun working together again on theatrical productions. I threw myself into organizing the wedding: a grand performance that I deliberately did not allow my mother to control. I refused to have the reception in her beautiful rose garden, which is what I knew she wanted—and what I asserted I did *not* want, even though I did. Absolutely miserable in this marriage from the get-go, I got into formal psychoanalysis. There would be another psychoanalyst when I eventually got divorced and moved.

Therapy was the religion of my family growing up. My uncle was a famous psychoanalyst. My mother had been analyzed by another famous psychoanalyst. Therapy was presented in the movies of the times as the miraculous talking cure. To question its value was to be a heretic. My father, asserted my mother after her second glass of wine, had never done enough therapy and therefore had not resolved his issues with his impossible mother, which explained why everything had gone wrong in their marriage. If religion traced sin back to Eve's disobedience, the psychological creation myth was that each person's fundamental unhappiness originated in the womb. My mother blamed her mother who had been indoctrinated into a culture of blaming her mother in between electric shock treatments. I blamed my mother. Movies and television and literature routinely made the mother—the overbearing mother, the neglectful mother, the narcissistic mother, the addicted mother, the helicopter mother, the single mother, the smothering mother—the scapegoat for the entire culture's neurosis.

Over the years I developed a well-honed litany of all of my mother's various hang-ups, failures, and misdemeanors to explain why I was so anxious and dissatisfied in my life.

She left me with an endless ever-changing stream of teenage babysitters. She bemoaned that her mother had abandoned her to a formal nanny who brought her down from the nursery at cocktail hour for a daily audience with her parents. But at least she'd had a consistent caretaker, I complained. I couldn't keep these girls straight when I was little. I loved some of them, but they all disappeared after a summer or a season. I hated others, but they disappeared too. Everyone disappeared—especially my mother: to another dinner party, a political event, the theater, a wine tasting. I wanted her to get on the floor and play with me. She never did. When I was old enough, ten or so, she just left me on my own, a TV dinner to heat up in the oven, a show to watch on TV, an empty house to wander through, early latchkey kid that I was.

When she was home, she had a tendency to collapse in front of me, wailing and crying. Christmas was too much for her. She couldn't do it this year. She just couldn't. "I can't . . . I can't do it . . . I can't do one more thing," she'd moan in a morass of self-pity. On a trip to England together when I was eleven, she had a total nervous breakdown at the hotel when they informed us that our room wasn't ready yet. The clerks were embarrassed for her; the other guests appalled. "No one loves me! No one loves me!" she wept. "C'mon Mum," I said, terrified to be in a foreign country alone with her. "Let's go sit in the park in the sun. Maybe we can get an ice cream or something."

Sugar was her love language. Specialty cookies brought back from her latest trip to the city. A pantry well-stocked with candies and chocolates to soothe myself with when I was alone. An open tab at the local general store where I could get unlimited pastries and doughnuts as I wandered around town with a friend. One day, as if seeing me for the first time, she asked, "Why are you so fat?" I had no answer for her, only shame. She was beautiful and I was not. Now I was a blight upon her charms.

As an adolescent I was determined to earn her attention. I dieted to anorexic perfection so that she bragged I wore size 2 jeans and rewarded me with a shopping trip to New York City. But then, paradoxically, she saw me as a rival. When a handsome married English teacher began dropping by with books for me to read in high school, slipping me love letters and trying to set up secret assignations that unnerved me, she turned on me one day in the kitchen without warning. "I know what you are up to. Don't you lead that man on. Don't you break up his marriage. I've got my eyes on you."

My father had left her, and she careened from raging fury to hopeless depression. In the morning before I left for school, I would make her coffee and bring her breakfast in the hope that she would feel loved enough to get out of bed and begin her day.

"I cannot make her feel loved enough," I told one therapist after another. "She is too needy. She is a bottomless pit of inconsolable need."

She did this. She did this. She didn't do this. If only she would go back to work, get remarried, do something that showed me how to claim power and purpose, hope and joy. If only she would claim her own joy. She wanted me to save her. I wanted her to save me and she couldn't. Hour after hour, session after session, year after year, I confirmed with whatever therapist I was seeing that my mother was the problem. If only I could extricate myself from the clinging tendrils of her dependency on me. Then I would finally feel better. Right?

We must heal the mother wound by becoming our own mothers. But what happens when we become more and more alienated from the very source of our belonging? Before and after therapy, I would often reward myself with sugary treats . . . craving sweetness, comfort, consolation, the breast, all that I was not actually getting from these high-priced sessions. No wonder so many of us, despite ever more therapy, feel worse and worse. No wonder so many of us are more and more addicted, more and more anxious and depressed, trying to fill up our empty souls with something, anything, other than our mothers.

At thirty I was living in the concrete wasteland of New York City feeling absolutely desolate. I had good friends, a good job, good enough dates. I meditated and went to aerobics classes. I paid my bills and went to therapy. But where was my home? Would I ever put down roots? Where did my bones belong?

I felt so stuck in my head, in my endless tiresome whir of unhappy thoughts. I talked endlessly about my problems and issues and never felt any different. One bleak day I decided I needed to break set, to do something I'd never done before, go outside of my routines and comfort zone. I needed some kind of vision quest to pit myself against the elements and figure out who I really was and what I really wanted. I wrote an essay and got a scholarship for a summerlong wilderness adventure in the Smoky Mountains. I trained for months in advance that spring, running through Riverside Park along the Hudson River after I was finished teaching for the day. I bought special socks and hiking boots. I booked my flights, made my plans. And then my mother was diagnosed with incurable lymphoma.

The oncologist gave her three months to live and did not advise treatment.

But my mother—who had been so defeated for so much of my life by my father's rejection of her—refused to accept the verdict of her diagnosis.

She told her doctor to treat her anyway, blast her with whatever radiation and chemicals he had at his disposal. "What's the worst that's going to happen? I'm going to die? But if there is any chance, no matter how slight, I might live long enough to hold at least one grandchild, then I'm going to do whatever I can."

Her surprising courage inspired my own. "You're going to beat this, Mum," I told her. "I can feel it. So I'm going on my trip. I need to. I have to make sense of things."

I was sitting on her bed beside her. Her back was already burned from treatment. Her hair had begun to fall out. She couldn't eat. She sighed deeply and stared out the window at the setting sun. On the one hand, she was reaching for a greater faith than reason allowed, and on the other, I knew she thought she might never see me again.

Still cancer had brought forth the expression of her deepest desire—for grandchildren, for descendants, for a family to remember her and her story. I hadn't known this until her cancer. I thought all she wanted was my father back. I thought she wanted me to move back home with her. I thought she wanted me to give her the love my father could not, and I felt trapped in a morass of confused blame and longing. But no, she wanted grandchildren. And I wanted children. We wanted the same thing after all. Her heart and my heart were not so different. And for reasons I could not articulate this trip was about ensuring that all of that happened.

"I'll write to you," I promised, uncertain how I'd mail my letters from the woods. "I'll be back in the middle of August."

I left her crying in her bed.

Of course, I worried that I'd made a selfish decision. Perhaps that guilt even propelled me to get whatever I could out of my adventure—the hiking, the white-water canoeing, the rock climbing. But I hadn't really thought through the rock climbing . . . I have always been terrified of heights, specifically bridges with low guardrails and ledges on the edge of cliffs. I am phobic about falling, which—given that I'm a bit of a klutz—is not entirely unwarranted. The first few days of my expedition we did some bouldering, which was bad enough, but on the third day we hiked up a steep mountain to confront, almost at the peak, a sheer rock face, hundreds and hundreds of feet high, overlooking a vast valley. Just looking at it activated my vertigo.

Our crew had two guides, a man and a woman, who led us through each challenge. But on this particular day there was also a rock-climbing expert to see to our safety. He was a young lean man in his early twenties with a mop of curly dark hair. He clambered up the rock face like a spider, hammering in pitons, securing ropes, showing us what we were going to do—how to secure a belay, how to use our feet and our hands, how to find the variations in the stone. One after another of my companions stepped forward, strapped themselves in, and ascended. The oldest woman among us carefully found a foothold and made her way up the rock face. The gym teacher from Canada quickly scrambled up as if he were taking the stairs two at a time. The young mom who insisted on carrying a makeup kit in her backpack and putting on lipstick each morning got up with no trouble at all. Finally, I was the only participant not at the summit. The counselors told me it was time to hitch myself in and get going.

I was out of my mind with fear just standing there on solid ground. It was too high up, too open; there was too much nothing in every direction. The thought of climbing up even higher made me want to throw up. I was already trembling as I clipped myself into the belay and tried to feel along the stone for some cleft of rock I could hold on to. I pressed my fingers into a small concavity and hauled myself upward. I pressed my toes into the wall. I could do this. I was strong and flexible. But I could not stop thinking about all of that empty air behind me, beneath me, stretching out all around me. I might disappear into that nothingness forever.

I've never cried easily. My mother always said I was her easiest baby, which meant that I learned quickly that it was pointless to waste energy calling for someone who might never come. That was the parenting wisdom of the times: don't be indulgent or they'll never stop whining. So I was pretty tough. I didn't cry when someone hurt my feelings or when I was disappointed or angry. I didn't cry at sad movies or when my first marriage ended. But on that rock wall, halfway up, clinging to the stone like a bit of lichen, I began to bawl. I was weeping, big gulping sobs. I was too scared to shimmy myself down hundreds of feet, and I was too petrified to move up any higher toward the faraway summit. I could not traverse another hundred feet into the air. I could not. I didn't care that everyone was watching me. I didn't care that I was failing publicly. Some people talk about hitting rock bottom as the worst thing that ever happened to them. For me it was hitting rock halfway up.

My companions called down encouragement from the top. My counselors called up reassurance from below. But I could not move. I was hyperventilating, certain I was going to pass out and fall to my death. I couldn't see because I was crying so hard. I couldn't go down; I couldn't go up. I was completely stuck. I had never been so nakedly panicked, as if the hot magma of existential anxiety I had always felt at my core had finally exploded through my whole being. I was volcanic with terror. I fantasized about rescue helicopters arriving to pluck me from the side of the mountain. Or maybe I would just burst a blood vessel, throw an embolism, have a heart attack, and die. Anything would be preferable to this.

"Hey," said a quiet voice, the gentleness of his tone cutting through the incessant cheerleading from above and below.

The young rock-climbing expert, the belay rope in his hands, was staring at me, just feet from the faraway summit. I was sure he thought I was a tiresome toddler, a mountaineering failure, a total drag on the day's adventure. But his face showed no judgment, only curiosity.

"Can you hear me?" he said without raising his voice.

I nodded, hiccuping back my sobs.

"I want you to take your right hand and let go of the rock and hold the rope. Can you do that?"

"I'll fall!" I wailed.

"I'm going to hold you," he said evenly. "The rope is going to hold you. I've got you."

I began blubbering again.

"I've got you. Let go."

It took me ten minutes, but finally I let go with one hand, and then, with his patient encouragement, with the other. I let go of the rock, of my fear, of everything, and I clutched that rope for dear life. It wasn't so much about letting go but about holding on—and knowing that I was held.

"See," he grinned. "I've got you. You can't fall when the rope connects us."

He had me. The rope had me. I was perfectly safe.

I waited for him to haul me up the mountain, but nothing happened.

"Now," he said. "You've got to climb. Take your hands off the rope and begin climbing."

I looked up at him again. The sun was behind him, bronzing his dark curls. He was smiling, but he also was serious.

"I'm still scared," I whispered.

"Sure," he said. "Of course you are."

I made it to the top of the mountain before sunset, and everyone hugged me and cheered for me. Nothing I'd ever achieved in my life had ever felt more powerful. The young man, whose name I couldn't remember even a day later, winked at me. After we had all rappelled back down the mountain to begin the long hike back to camp, I turned to thank him, but he'd already disappeared into the forest, probably off to a bar for a drink with his friends. I never saw him again, this young man who taught me the deepest lesson of all about what it means to be a mother.

Later that night we all sat around the campfire, singing songs and telling stories, the dark at our backs. I'd never felt so intimate and safe with a group of people before—because I'd been able to show them how scared I really was. Over the next weeks each of us would come up against our fears. The gym teacher was unexpectedly terrified of white water, the middle-aged woman of thunderstorms. The woman with the makeup kit was scared of nothing and gave us all makeovers one bleak rainy day. We held on to each other and found ways to feel the threads of connection holding us, entangling us, reassuring us. We walked through the woods together, often quietly, and slept beside each other at night. I wondered if this was not what our most ancient ancestors experienced, a small band of kin, all mothers, holding each other in different ways at different times.

So many of us are disappointed and frustrated, if not infuriated, by our mothers within the empires of patriarchy. We ache for something they have not given us or done for us. But what if the problem with civilization is not the failures of our individual mothers but that we no longer have *enough* mothers to guide us through the different ordeals, struggles, and possibilities of a life? Civilization has systematically cut the many umbilical cords that connect us to all of our mothers—our plant and animal mothers, our mothers from past lives, our stone and mountain mothers. I went to therapy because I had not received the mothering I needed, but instead of feeling the ropes that connected me to all of the many mothers of my soul, I became more and more estranged from the only mother I had. I was left dangling in midair.

Is it any wonder that we need ever-stronger drugs to manage our anxieties and depressions? Because we do not feel attached, we reach for something, anything, to hold on to—power or money, fantasies or addictions. But what if we could feel again the etheric cords that anchor us to the earth and to each other?

I returned from my wilderness adventure having received such powerful mothering that I was ready to be a mother myself. I came home and cared for my mother, who was unexpectedly, miraculously, responding to the treatment, with a newfound tenderness. I sought out experiences in nature that gave me the mothering I craved. I met a man who loved to be outdoors as much as I did and who offered to me gentle reassurances to begin taking my writing seriously. I got pregnant and had my first baby. We moved together out of the city to a little run-down moss-covered cottage in Woodstock where the black bears circled our house at dusk and the owls called to us throughout the night.

Becoming an actual mother was overwhelming—physically, emotionally, spiritually, and practically. I promised my daughter that first night I held her, the snow falling softly outside the hospital window, that I would be the best mother the world had ever known—still not really understanding that mothering was something no individual could accomplish on their own.

I had to go back to work when my daughter was three months old so we could keep our health insurance, pay the bills, cover the babysitter. I was exhausted physically from nursing and being up all night. I had a pile of baby books by the bed but no cohort of women circling me with advice and care. My own mother was still getting chemo. Besides, she kept telling me that I needed to learn to let the baby cry and get over herself. I found myself envying her ability to just be a mother and not have to also hold down a job at the same time. Clark was an incredibly loving man, but he'd been raised down south and so much of what women did—from homemaking to childcare—was absolutely invisible to him.

My mother's intermittent nervous breakdowns, the list of babysitters on the bulletin board, and even the sugary rewards began to make more sense to me. Still, it took me a long time to see the architecture of this impossible situation, to realize how the entire edifice of civilization was built atop isolating and blaming the mother for everything that went wrong. Ashamed and defeated, I fell back on the usual scapegoat—my own mother. It was her fault that I was not adequately prepared for this role. It was her fault I was frazzled. If only she were younger and healthier. If only she could help me out financially. If only she knew anything about how to be a good mother.

I longed for a mother I didn't have. In one of the children's books I read to my daughter, a little bird falls out of the nest and hops around the yard asking various animals and inanimate objects, "Are you my mother?" As a young mother, I felt like that lost little bird, desperate for the mothering that would help me be a mother.

That is when I first began calling out to the dead at night when I felt hopeless and scared, on the way home from work as the subway rumbled through tunnels underground, whenever I felt untethered and alone. "Are you my mother?" I began asking the darkness itself. I longed to feel some tug on the other end of my soul.

One afternoon after a long day while both kids ran in circles around me, hollering, I begged them, "Please be quieter: I'm at the end of my rope."

Sophie stopped and stared at me, wide-eyed. "Can I play with the end of your rope?"

Despite myself, I burst out laughing and pulled her onto my lap. Of course she could.

But I was less and less generous with my own mother. Soon after we'd moved to Woodstock, she decided that she wanted to sell the house she'd built with my father, where I'd grown up, to move next door to me and Clark. My first response, straight from the heart, was elation. This was what families were supposed to do. The kids could spend afternoons gardening with her while I wrote. They could snuggle with her and watch old movies together and eat chocolates. They could have an old granny who lived up the road to confide in and tell their secrets.

An older woman I respected, a therapist, warned me that I shouldn't do this. "Your mother is a narcissist. She is going to demand to be at the center of your life." A local friend of mine, alienated from her own mother, asked me if I could "be myself" around my mother. I wasn't sure that I could. But then I wasn't sure who I really was either—some days I felt like a bread-baking hippie mother, others a frustrated artist, and still others like just another stressed-out parent. At this time, Sophie was obsessed with *The Little Mermaid*. It was the only movie she would watch. "That's my mother," I said to Clark about the character Ursula. "She's a big bosomy bossy impossible sea witch. Do you think she's going to steal my voice?"

I wish I had known in those days how to summon the counsel of the dead and hear their guidance. I wish I had known that the great mother goddess Tiamat was a sea witch vilified through the millennia, her very body severed from the bodies of her daughters. I wish I had trusted my heart and my intuition. But, instead, I listened to my fears and to conventionality. I called up my mother, after she was already working with a real estate agent and had told all of her friends she was moving to Woodstock, and announced that I could not have her living so close to me. "It's not going to work," I said bluntly.

I believe in sin, not as a "missing of the mark" as some people claim, but as a choice, a mistake, that haunts our souls for lifetimes. This was one of my sins: telling my mother that she could not be close to her kin. I denied her access to the grandchildren for whom she had fought and survived. This she did not fight. "Yes, yes," she said, coldly, resigned to yet another inevitable betrayal.

A few weeks later she sold our childhood home anyway to some rich lawyers from Boston and bought a little cottage across from the highway in her town. She gave away all of her beloved plants, the ones she'd nursed and loved for decades. She told us to take the paintings and books we wanted and donated the rest to the library. She handed us each a box filled with memorabilia. She got rid of her life. The whole experience felt terrible and final.

Immediately her health began to deteriorate. She became disoriented and forgetful, which in the beginning I was sure was because she was drinking more. But then she was diagnosed with congestive heart failure as a result of chemotherapy and was in and out of the hospital. The doctors began to suspect she had a vascular dementia. We hired a woman to care for her, but Mum wouldn't let her into the house and accused her of stealing. She began showing up for appointments at all hours and forgetting how to find her way home. Within a year we had packed up her things and moved her in to live with us after all.

My children remember it as a charmed time. They often crawled into bed with their grandmother and snuggled close to her. They ate rice pudding together after school and my mother read them picture books on the couch. Later Sophie would say that she could tell Gammy Pat anything, everything, and it was safe because she didn't remember any of it. I would wonder forever after what might have happened if she had moved to Woodstock with her own home. Might she have rallied instead of deteriorated? Might she have lived longer?

She died a year after she moved in with us, when I was forty-one.

I had wasted precious time in my twenties raging against my mother in therapy. I wish I had known then how to summon the ancestral grandmothers to help us heal our relationship. I imagine a circle of old wisewomen around us, guiding us. One would help us recover from our addictions—mine to sugar and hers to alcohol. Another would sort through our dreams for wisdom about our soul entanglements through other lifetimes. What traumas were we reenacting from past incarnations? One might have cast the runes or read the tarot. One of the old women would tell us to stop talking so much and remember how to dance together. I imagine thirteen old grandmothers, one for each of the moons, each with a different gift, circling us the way the fairies had circled the baby's bassinet in *Sleeping Beauty*. What if we had both felt sufficient mothering—not from each other but from the dead?

What if we could ask of every being we meet, "Are you my mother?" and know that the answer would always be yes, that there was not a single mother, a perfect mother, just for us, but a world that was nothing but mothers who had loved us and could guide us through the depths of time?

We interred my mother's ashes in the town graveyard. It felt arbitrary. She had purchased a plot in a gorgeous cemetery near Boston where some of her best friends were buried but, unsentimentally, she'd sold it toward the end. She'd thrown her own mother's ashes into the sea. Mum had never felt like she truly belonged in her New England town, and none of us lived nearby. Still, we wanted a place to go and pay homage to the body that had borne us. We opened the urn and mixed her ashes with the sandy soil. We had a gravestone commissioned. Once or twice a year we came on pilgrimage with flowers. Yet visiting her grave, I felt nothing. Her bodily remains might be under the grass on the edge of a scrub pine forest, but my mother was somewhere else.

On one visit, some years after she'd passed, I decided I wanted to show the kids the house where I'd grown up, surrounded by the gardens my mother had tended so lovingly. Maybe the new owners would let us come in and look around. Would any of the roses still be there? As we pulled off the road, I was struck by the neglect—the gravel driveway was filled with weeds, the rhododendrons had not been pruned, and ivy was creeping all over the house.

"It doesn't look like anyone's here, but if there is, I'll explain who I am," I said as I got out of the car.

"Of course," agreed Clark. "I'm sure the owners will understand."

When they built the house, my parents had taken the giant glacial stones unearthed from the foundation and arranged them like paleolithic cairns along the driveway. The path curved around them toward the back of the house, and as I turned the corner, I saw that the roses were in full bloom. The ornamental pines had sent branches swooping across the yard. The herb garden by the kitchen had gone wild. The daisies and bee balm had spread beyond their borders. It was all as I had remembered it—only wilder, stranger, and even more beautiful.

I knocked on the door, and there was no answer. I knocked again and then walked fully around to the back of the house. From the road the house had no windows, but the other three sides were nothing but glass. I could see completely inside and was stunned to discover that every room was empty. No furniture, no art, no plants, no lamps even. No one was living there. The people who bought the house must have purchased it for their retirement, I thought, or maybe as an investment. Maybe they were about to sell it to someone else. But every time I visited the house in subsequent years, it was still empty and the gardens were more and more overgrown. The roof seemed in good repair and the path to the kitchen door was clear, so it was being maintained at some level. But no one was living there.

Except for my mother, of course.

I could feel her presence—tending, coaxing, and encouraging the gardens that she had loved. I could feel my grandmother there, too, in the pink tea roses climbing up the wall. The forget-me-nots, now going to seed, had all come from her home. To call the place haunted felt both accurate and imprecise because the ghosts were so astoundingly present and alive. Twenty years after my mother's death the house would still be empty and the gardens ever exultant. I visited the house even in my dreams—as if it were a magical portal to other worlds.

In one of these dreams I walked through my mother's house and came to an apartment building where a motherly woman and a young girl were punching numbers on a key code to let themselves into a building. I slipped in, invisibly, behind them. I walked down a narrow hallway, noting the kitchen, the closets, the wood paneling, until I came to a small balcony overlooking a beach. Now my mother was standing beside me. She sighed and I felt so many things . . . that she was living here but that she did not want to live here, that she had resigned herself to living here because I had not wanted her to live near me.

I woke up certain of two things: One was that I had been given a glimpse of my mother in another incarnation. I was almost certain that she was the little girl I had seen. And the other was that many years ago when I had first gotten into therapy, my first utterance had not been a Freudian slip after all.

"I was forty-two when my mother was born," I said out loud beside Clark in bed.

"Right," said Clark, blearily, reaching for his glasses. How many times had he heard me retell this story?

"But my mother was forty-one when I was born. Not forty-two," I explained.

"Okay. Meaning?"

"I was forty-one when my mother died at the end of May, and I would have been forty-two nine months later. I was forty-two when my mother was born: when she was *reborn*. The first thing I said in therapy wasn't a mistake but a prophecy."

Clark went downstairs to get some coffee. "What does all this mean?" he said at last, after he'd drunk half a cup.

"Remember how in Tibetan Buddhism each Dalai Lama leaves signs and sends dreams to help the other lamas find his newest incarnation? I think the details in my dream will help me recognize my mother come back. And I think . . ." I paused to take a deep breath before sharing an assertion for which I had no proof, only heart certainty. "I think I will have an opportunity to make amends to my mother. Either I will help her heal with her mother in this new life or I will insist that she come and live with us for some reason I can't even imagine. Or maybe she will offer me some kind of mothering I need. I don't know how it will play out: it's a mystery. But as you often say, there are no single outcome scenarios. No story is ever over once we claim the long story. There is always enough time for reunions, healing, and love."

I will meet my mother again, in this life, but how and when I do not know. Will I smell her, see her, touch her, recognize her by some indefinable something—a gesture, a spark—that is a sign only to me? Maybe she will be a friend's daughter. Maybe she will be my own granddaughter. But I do know that she is guiding me to her—and this time I will not let resentments or frustrations stand between the intimacy and power of our connection and our long soul story together through the depths of deep time.

# A Message from the Last Daughter at the End of the World

Look at me.

I stand with my hands outstretched, my eyes downcast, veiled, and seemingly compliant. I am alone. No one remembers the names of my grandmothers, disappeared in the dust of time. I have been separated from my many mothers through the ages. How much easier it is to frighten me, abuse me, and control me without these circles of protection.

You think you know who I am. You've all seen those robed and veiled images of the Virgin Mary, mass-produced in plaster and plastic. They depict me as barely a teenager. Beneath my pastel coverings you cannot tell if I really have a body. Certainly if I do, it does not stink or bleed or grow curly hairs in private places. I am brought to you as a good girl and not a woman. I am brought to you as a pure and holy image of submission to the divine.

Once your people made images of their grandmothers' bodies to hold in their hands. They wanted to remind themselves of where they came from and who loved them. They loved the breasts that had suckled generations of children, the bellies that had borne their mothers, the legs, the hips, the buttocks of these old women who were mirrors of the mountains and the trees and the stones. Each of these figurines was fashioned from the memory of a real woman, a beloved old one—some of them were wide, some were thin, all were grounded with age. These people, your ancestors, looked upon the naked bodies of their grandmothers not with disgust but devotion. These grandmothers circled the mothers who circled their daughters with protection.

Even when they had been cast aside, people still saw the bodies of their mothers as holy. Their Madonnas bared their breasts to nurse their children.

They stood with jaunty hips to hold their toddlers steady. They were real women, too, modeled on real women, mothers the artists had known, who could look you in the eye and wink. They stared straight at you, daring anyone to defy their power and their joy. They knew how to birth a life, a world, a cosmos.

In the modern age all that you have left is me: a girl, seemingly without desire or passion or will, awaiting her orders, ready to listen to God, painted pale blue like a pill given to her by a doctor who wants her to forget her pain. I ask you to see what I am hiding beneath these robes—how my body has been violated, polluted, raped, and tormented through the ages. Look at what civilization does to your girls, how you treat them, how you hurt them. Do I have track marks up my arms from my attempts to quell my own agony, scars on my thighs from where I cut myself to manage my desolation? Lift my robes and look at me. Bear witness, if you can, to what has happened to all of your daughters.

And know that even so here I am, here I stand, at the end of the world. Nothing can defile me. Nothing can destroy me. When the ages have covered over your monuments and museums, when your roads and wires are buried beneath time, when your words and achievements are forgotten, I will still be here, standing, waiting, praying that you remember who I really am.

When a hurricane levels a neighborhood, leaving behind a wasteland of debris, I stand amid the ruins unharmed. A fire blazes through a region, burning homes and forests to the ground, and there I am, defiant amid the ashes. People wear an image of me around their neck, the Miraculous Medal, and know that even though I am all that is left—I am everything.

Who do you think I *am*?

I gave birth to my own mother, I died, and I was reborn as her daughter.

The old ones and the young ones are the same ones.

If you want to find me, seek out your daughters and listen to their stories. Seek out your daughters even now, your daughters unable to show their faces, your daughters starving themselves to death to keep looking like girls, your daughters enslaved in brothels and slums and factories around the world, your daughters whose bodies are filled with toxins and poisons, your daughters who carry pepper spray in their pockets and trauma in their souls. Seek out your daughters who are terrified, defeated, enraged, depressed, undone by anxiety, and know that unless these girls are left standing the world cannot be reborn.

You are their circle of protection. You are *my* circle of protection.

The grandmothers, the mothers, and the daughters are the protectors of the Earth.

I am the Earth.

Come. Look at that popular image of the one you call the Virgin Mary again. Really look at it. Look at how she appears on the Miraculous Medal. Look at the diamond shape of her body, the folds of her robe, the small round orb of her head. Do you know what you are seeing? Yes, you do. Of course you do.

I am the great portal of all life, the pathway to the womb through which flow the salty waters of desire. I am the vulva at the heart of the world. When everything has fallen to pieces, after the floods and the winds and the fire, after the towers have all fallen, I will always give birth to another world.

This is where you come from. This is how you will all come back.

# An Invitation: Summoning the Hidden Power of Our Ancestral Mothers

How do we give our ancestors back the complexity of their stories, their lived reality, and their overlooked powers? We know so little about so many of them, especially the women. Sometimes all we have is a single story or a banal fact. Yet with our intuition and imagination, we can begin to spin from even the most delicate thread all that has been forgotten. Each of us is psychic, whether we acknowledge it or not, and the ancestors are waiting to inspire us.

If all we know is that this old grandmother made quilts, we can imagine how she might help us piece together our lives. If this ancient aunt traveled across an ocean on her own, she is who we can call on for courage. If our mothers and grandmothers were victims of trauma and violence, they are uniquely aware of how to help us avoid danger and oppression.

Nothing is coincidental. The little we know is exactly what we need to summon our oldest mothers.

## *Let the Healing Begin*

- Find the name of a woman who died as a slave, a witch, or vilified by the patriarchy. She might be biologically related to you—or she might have been an Indigenous woman murdered near where you now live, a woman enslaved where you grew up, a woman tortured and killed in the land of your ancestors. Most of all, let your intuition guide you to the woman who needs to be remembered.

- Say her name out loud. This is your most powerful spell. This woman is your protector and your guide and your mother. She has known the worst that patriarchy can do to us, and she is ready to guide our empowerment and our healing. If you are scared or anxious, call on her. The dead no longer need healing; they have recovered the long story of their souls. They are ready to repair the world.

- Make a doll, a poppet, to represent her on your altar. Often, in an age before photography, women made little dolls to help them remember those they loved on the other side. They took twigs and wove them together with twine and thread. A bit of wool became some hair. They had only to gather a little bit of this and a little bit of that to make a magic portal to the land of the dead. Create your protector out of the detritus and remains of your life. Go outside and gather branches, fronds of ferns, dried wildflowers and herbs, feathers, shells, stones, acorns, and seeds. Weave sticks together with thread or yarn to give her arms and legs. Dry an apple for her head. Make her body from a corn husk. Decorate her with old bits of cloth, buttons, leftover earrings, a broken necklace. You do not need to buy anything to make her. She is already in your life and ready to come into being.

- To hold these dolls is to summon the magic from our ancestral grandmothers. Children hold poppets as they fall asleep and take so many forgotten mothers into their dreams. Make yourself a mother to hold in your hand, to hold on to when you are frightened, and to bring to you the wisdom and guidance you need for your life. Now you know her name. Say it out loud as your mantra.

## *The Oracle of Our Grandmothers*

- Create an oracle deck for your grandmothers, aunties, and beloveds on the other side. Each card is dedicated to one particular ancestral figure. Decide what this person's greatest gift might be. If they were a musician, perhaps they are the goddess of finding a voice. If they were a gardener, they could be the patron saint of coming into bloom. If they had a string of unwanted pregnancies, put them in charge of birth control. You get to decide.

- Imagine what symbols you want connected with these guardians. Is your grandmother associated with a particular place or object? Collage these cards and add objects that reveal their talents and interests. You may also want to think of these mothers as "not just a human being." Maybe this person is also a crow, or a seal, or a black cat. Remember the witches were often accused of shape-shifting, of becoming animals. Let's allow them to be animals again.

- Choose one of your grandmothers and give her back her story. You may have to imagine most of it from a few pieces of paltry information. Trust your intuition. You may have to shift perspective profoundly. How can you retell the stories of your ancestors so that they have their power returned to them? Eventually you may want to create a book of such stories to accompany your deck.

- Your deck will grow. Trust the process. Move slowly. When you need help, pull a card and see who shows up. You will get to know these mothers intimately by doing so.

- Eventually, you will become the memory keeper for these ancestors. One day you will pass along the deck to someone younger. Or perhaps you will make it as a gift to share with family members. You will transform your family story as you tell new stories about the miracles these beloveds on the other side have brought to you all.

## *Healing with Our Mothers*

- Take some quiet time. Light a candle. Make a cup of tea. Put on soothing music. Now let yourself feel all of your feels. You do not have to perform your goodness or your worthiness. You just have to access your authentic emotions. Answer the following three questions without any thinking or planning. Just write. Write for five minutes in response to each question. Just write.
    - *How did your mother disappoint you?*
    - *How did your mother frustrate you?*
    - *How did your mother infuriate you?*

- Now ask yourself a final question: *What do you need to heal?* Even if it feels impossible—*especially* if it feels impossible—write about what you need and want. What do you want for yourself, for this relationship? If your mother is on this side of the veil, certain things will feel possible and certain things will feel impossible. Similarly, if your mother is deceased, certain things will feel possible but others will seem impossible. Don't worry about any of this. Nothing is impossible for the dead.

- Circle yourself with your many mothers—your animal mothers, your witch mothers, your earth mothers, your grandmothers. Summon them by name. You may want to create a special place on your altar for your petition. You may want a small daily ritual of petitioning those on the other side for this help. You are asking them to be midwives of the miraculous and heal your relationship with your mother. You are asking them for what you want.

- The dead can see in the ten directions. They can see many different possibilities, many different unfoldings—and they have all the time in the world. The answers and solutions and magic they offer to you may be unexpected. It will arrive in its own time, in good time, in their time, in the right time and the right way. Trust the magic of these mothers.

- To express our gratitude to our mothers, we can tell our miracle stories to our friends and family. We can go on pilgrimage to their birthplaces and burial spots to say thank you. We can make art or write a song to honor what has happened. Most of all, we should ask for more, and stay in relationship with those who love us.

Our ancestral mothers are the medicine to heal the wounded heart of the world. We will know this is true the moment we begin asking for their help.

THE THIRD PART

# OUR MOTHERS *after* PATRIARCHY

## Chapter Seven

# A FOUNDATION OF FAITH

The idea of praying for material things that we need can feel spiritually unevolved. We should be praying for world peace, or at least something lofty like divine acceptance and personal liberation. Not my will but thy will be done after all. Isn't it crass to pray for *things*, like a job or a raise or a car?

It can certainly feel that way in many spiritual settings—where participants often outdo each other to perform their mystic worthiness or holy enlightenment.

But if we don't have a job, if we don't have enough money, if we don't have access to public transportation, seemingly mundane prayers might be essential to our very survival. If we have responsibilities for children and old folk, the sick and the disabled, our prayers for what we need to get through each day may be supporting not only us but all those in the orbit of our care. And those people who learn how to pray in those everyday moments of crisis and need are often the ones who know best how to navigate the most calamitous of situations when all hope seems lost. They have built a foundation of faith beneath them, everyday petition by everyday petition.

It is often invisible privilege that lets us not have to pray for stuff. We don't have to worry about where our next meal is coming from or how to keep a roof over our head or how to pay the bills or what it might cost to see the doctor.

I know a very devout Buddhist monk who has no pockets in his robes because he never touches money. This seemed very noble—until I noticed how this lifestyle of nonattachment was supported by a network of rich donors who flew him around the world for his various teaching gigs, arranged in advance for his cars and drivers, and saw to the maintenance of his austere but very elegant monastery. *Someone* was going to the grocery store—usually a woman—and coming back to the kitchen to prepare his meals, just like I did when he visited us, worried about the added expense to our monthly bills. Those hardworking women in the kitchens of various religious institutions are often praying very differently than the priests promenading in their robes. They are worried about their knees giving out and no longer being able to support their families. They are worried about the grandson smoking too much pot, about the neighbor always yelling at her child, about what a hard time their husband is having getting up the stairs these days. These old busybodies don't let go of anything—or anyone. These women stir the pot and fret about everything. And their fretting is prayer at its most fundamental.

When we fret, we turn something over and over in our minds repetitively. We anxiously worry a problem, sighing, shaking our heads, our hearts heavy. But to fret is also to make music with the strings of an instrument. To fret is to weave fibers into wool with our fingers. Our fretting can be a creative act as we untangle knots, wear away problems, spin new possibilities into being, and bring forth a new song. Our busy, fretting minds are also creative, imaginative minds turning straw into gold.

But we must remember that we are not fretting all by ourselves. The strings we hold and the threads we weave connect us to all other beings on this side of the veil and on the other. Each of our many worries—both trivial and profound—is an opportunity to connect with all the many beings who have mothered us through the ages.

Some years ago during a family holiday, my old couch bought before I got married finally collapsed. It had been used as a trampoline and turned into forts, comforted kids home sick from school, and been shredded by generations of cats. Its slipcover was long gone; the stuffing was fluffing out of various holes; and it had developed a musty smell that wouldn't go away. Then my niece sat on it and her butt went right to the ground. It had finally died. Clearly, it was time to get a new couch, but money was especially tight in those days. I checked out Freecycle online and various thrifting websites, but the available couches—most of them in acrylic plaid—seemed to be in even worse shape than mine.

The next morning Clark and I began our day as we always do: fretting and calling upon the dead for help. We sipped our coffee as the sun rose and watched the goldfinches at the feeder. I asked Clark's long-lived grandmother to make sure he ate better. I asked my father's medical secretary to help me get a doctor's appointment. I asked my mother's bossy Irish nanny Marie who kept everyone in line to help me with a firm email I needed to send.

Each day we summon all of our ancestors, all of our mothers from the other side, and give them their assignments. This is our daily ritual.

There are those we assign daily annoyances and others working on big intractable problems. We call upon family members, pets, neighbors, saints both traditional and secular, and random people who pop into our mind for no seeming reason.

On the morning after my couch collapsed, I called on my mother from this lifetime. "Mum," I said out loud, "I need your help. I need a new couch."

My mother's couch had been her throne. Surrounded by ferns and ficus trees, girded by bookshelves, it was the seat of her soft powers. It was long and wide, squishy with goose-down pillows, and covered in a velvety moss green corduroy. My mother stretched out on her couch at the end of the day, the newspaper at her side, a cat or two on her belly, and we visited with her there, offering up our confidences. When we moved away and came back home, our destination was the couch at her side. Over the years all of her children made love with someone after some party or other on that couch. Litters of kittens were born underneath it. That couch was my mother's great green womb from which the life of her family blossomed.

She'd had it hauled off to the dump when she sold the house because she said it was no longer worth redoing. "It's about to go," she said ruefully. "Just like me."

Now I was calling out to her. I needed something more than a piece of furniture: I needed my home's hearth space where my kin could gather and feel close. I wanted it to be a place for love and stories and joy. And I needed it to be affordable. Of course, if I'd had extra money in the bank, I might not have called on my mother. But that is why those without financial resources often know so much more about the economy of prayer than those with disposable income.

That day we drove confidently to every Goodwill and ReStore in the county. What we discovered was that there were a lot of ugly couches out there, and even the cheap ones felt too expensive. "I want a couch, Mum," I clarified out loud, Clark as my witness, "but I want a nice couch."

That winter my daughter, chronically ill, was going regularly to a number of different doctors the next town over. I would often swing past one of the local thrift stores as we drove back home. The hideous colors, the unnatural fabrics, the clunky designs, and the price tags all made me despair. Sophie, who loves to thrift for clothes, began begging after each appointment that we stop in one particularly funky junk shop on the wrong side of the local highway.

"They don't have furniture," I explained to her, not wanting to make that tricky left turn across traffic. "Besides they leave all their donations outside to get wet and moldy. We don't want to go there."

"They have clothes inside," she told me. "I want a better pair of jeans."

"Everything there looks disgusting," I said, vetoing her again. "Besides, you have a million pairs of jeans already."

Sophie shrugged, irritated. She felt terrible, and I was making her feel worse. Our relationship was fraying from an illness that was increasingly unmanageable. She was trusting the doctors less and less, and that scared me as we had no idea how to navigate her many physical challenges. We often fought these days.

I soothed myself by fantasizing about the brand-new slipcovered couch I wanted. How could I ever get the extra money for such a purchase? I was already working round the clock and caring for a sick child. I sighed. If only I could win the lottery, I thought, invoking that great substitute for prayer that the devotion to money calls forth from within us.

But I didn't buy a lottery ticket, and with each passing week, I had less money to spend on a couch. I felt more and more disgruntled about the available options. We couldn't even afford to have our old couch hauled off to the dump, so it sat there, broken, in the middle of the living room reminding me of how impossible life was beginning to feel.

The months passed, and I found myself browsing fancy furniture sites online, self-pitying and resentful. I gave up hope that I would ever have a couch again and stopped insisting we check out the ReStore on the way back from the doctor's.

"If we aren't going there, can we at least stop at that junk store?" Sophie asked. "Finally?"

"Let her stop," said Clark, who was with us that day.

"You never know," said Sophie.

You never know.

To pray is to step inside the mystery of all that we do not know. We pray because we have come to the end of our rope and we don't know what to do. Still, it is so hard to give up our desire to control and plan and manage how our lives will unfold. But to acknowledge the vast mysteries that surround us in every direction means we never know how our prayers will be answered or when—only that they will be.

I sighed, relenting. "All right. But we're not spending hours trying on clothes, okay?"

We took a left through speeding traffic and drove into the parking lot filled with rusty furnaces, broken picture frames, and boxes of old books.

Sophie was just about to get out of the car when a pickup truck pulled in beside us. In the flatbed, impossible to miss, was a beautiful red slipcovered couch. It looked brand-new. Amazed, I rolled down the window. "Are you dropping that off?" I asked incredulously. "How much?"

One of the guys shrugged. "Ninety bucks sound okay? But we'll deliver it and we'll get rid of your old couch if you have one. We were just going to leave this here as a donation after all."

I was speechless. Sophie was triumphant. "I told you so!" she said. I hadn't seen her so happy in months.

In that moment my mother answered many prayers simultaneously. I got my couch; the guys got ninety unexpected dollars; and my daughter got to prove me wrong. Or rather, more powerfully, my daughter got to prove me wrong about her intuition. Despite all evidence to the contrary, she had led me to the place where I found my couch. She also had intuitions about her healing journey that defied the standard medical options, and I needed to learn to trust those, too. On that journey we would probably have to swerve across traffic going in the opposite direction to some pretty unlikely places.

My mother was present in that parking lot with us, smiling, delighted with herself, a little smug. There is no way I can prove this, but I also felt her telling me that she wished she had listened to *me* more, that the healing that had not happened between her and me when she was alive could still happen between me and my daughter. The couch was just the beginning.

I got out my wallet and handed the guys in the truck all my cash, which was—not surprisingly—just enough. Sophie found the perfect pair of jeans inside. On the way home I found myself crying. My mother had gifted me the exact couch of my dreams, and it was the cheapest couch I had seen anywhere. I'd only had to ask. I'd only had to wait. I'd only had to give up all expectations about how my miracle might unfold. For the magic to happen I'd only had to trust the mystery of it all.

Our most ancient ancestors long before civilization were in a constant state of prayer for food and shelter and safety. Those prayers were a conversation with the souls of all those who had come before them. They asked for help, and then they listened to their dreams, to the earth, and to their intuition for answers. This is how they knew how to find the herds and the flocks, the healing plants and bounteous berries. This is how they found love and renewal even amid calamities only written down in the geological record—the ice ages, the volcanic eruptions, the falling of the stars. They told and retold the stories of their ancestors who always helped them, and the memories of those actual grandparents and loved ones slipped into deep time, becoming more and more mythic with the passing years. Eventually they became those we call the immortal gods and goddesses. But in the beginning they were just the dead that the living called out to in desperation.

These ancient peoples still knew that every soul is immortal and woven together by unfathomable mysteries. They prayed to their great-grandmother, and a stranger arrived with a miracle. They prayed to an ancient aunt, and a child was born. They prayed to their forgotten mothers, and the whole Earth showed up to answer their prayers. The mountains and the stones, the trees and the flowers, the rivers and the rain, every animal and insect and fish and fungus had been a mother and would continue to be a mother to these people. The dead are the living; the living are the dead: it's all mothers in the ten directions, fretting and entangling our souls together with worries and care and love, weaving and unweaving and reimagining the entire fabric of reality.

But how do we live like this again, with our feet firmly grounded in this faith?

It is the small ordinary miracles of day-to-day life that give us the faith to pray for everything. When we truly know that the dead are real, that they are all our mothers that have ever been, we will move through the world very differently. A bill is paid, a crisis averted, a diagnosis found to be not as bad as we thought. We get an actual person on the other end of the phone. This is where faith starts.

It felt impossible to imagine that I could have a nice couch, but the guys pulled their truck in right behind our car and unloaded it as soon as we were home. It became a warm red heart in the center of my living room.

But I did not get my couch by overnight delivery. I did not open the catalog and pull out my credit card. I did not put the coin of prayer into a vending machine and grab the candy bar I'd chosen. I had to trust the timing, the process, the mysterious unfolding. It was no different with my daughter's illness. I would pray for her to heal, and I would have to trust the unfolding.

Each day our planet turns into darkness. Our lives are bordered by all that we do not know—what came before this life and what will come after. Every night when we sleep, we enter the dark realms for renewal. Our solar system circles through the cosmos. Most of the cosmos is dark matter, and even to the best scientists, that dark matter remains a mystery.

I have faith that my daughter will eventually be healed, but I also know that this may not happen in any way that I imagine. Every prayer is answered, but not every prayer is answered within a single life. Yet how many lifetimes did I pray for the blessings of *this* life? For reunion with my beloved husband and my children? For a life as a writer? To live in these mountains that haunt my dreams? How many lifetimes have I prayed to find my way back to these people, this place, this purpose? What prayers will I carry forward, lifetime upon lifetime?

How will this exhausted and depleted and poisoned planet heal? How will human beings surrender their addiction to civilization and supremacy? How will we again embrace the circle of mothers and the long story of their souls? What are we to do? How are we to go on?

It is those small daily experiences of care from my ancestral mothers that give me the faith to relax inside of all that I do not and may never know. Because I can entrust them with the smallest of problems, I also know they will see to my deepest desires. My fretting weaves me into an experience of belonging. That belonging itself is the answer to so many of our prayers.

And when we belong again to the eternal circle of mothers, when we feel mothered and loved and seen and known by all that is, only then can we become the mothers the world needs us to be.

# A Message from the Mothers of the Miraculous

When a black hole swallows a star, it is praying for a cosmos. When the sunlight falls across the body of the ocean, sinking into its dark depths, it is dreaming of a great green world, of trees reaching up their arms to the sky, the birds singing in the sunrise, a child standing in a golden beam at the edge of the forest. That forest grew from the lichen on a rock that prayed to be worn down by the rain and become soil, layers of life and death and rot through epochs and ages, that would one day hold a seed that would pray to find its way through the soil to the sunlight. Every soul is yearning for another soul—for the ecstasies of touch, the intimacies of mingling, the revelations of transformation. What bodies will we become next? Every prayer is answered by the birth of the unexpected. Every prayer gives birth to a miracle.

We cannot imagine a child before the child is born. We cannot imagine the sound of their voice, their first words, their adolescent rage, the desperate longings of their soul, their disappointments and failures, their tragedies and trauma, their talents and their gifts, the wild seeds in their heart that need a wildfire before they can crack open and grow. When this child is in the world, we cannot imagine the world without them. This child becomes our world, and the world becomes something else.

No wonder prayer can feel so frightening and dangerous. Nothing will ever be the same again.

Love is what guides us through these changes and revolutions. We call out to our beloved, and our beloved becomes our child becomes our mother becomes another cosmos becomes a star who surrenders to the embrace of the darkness and gives birth to a universe. Where does love begin? Where does love end? Trace a circle—of our sun through the spirals of the Milky Way, of our round moon around the fecund Earth, from one warm season to another of cold; trace the whorls on a tree or a shell, and know that there is no beginning and no end to a soul. There is only the calling and the return, the loving and the departure, the eternal romance, the mystic dance of the heart. Every body is always changing—from seed to sprout to fruit, from infant to toddler to elder, from one life to another. Love is what endures through the eons.

The shell washed back and forth by the tides is slowly worn away into sand that sinks beneath the weight of the ocean, becoming hard and still, becoming stone, that rises as the Earth shifts its plates, becomes a small rock bound by roots, that emerges to the air again after the storm washes away the dirt on the mountain. You come up the path and see it lying there—a small rock that has the shape of a woman—and you lean down and take it into your hands and remember a mother from so long ago that there are no words to describe all that you were to each other. How long have you been calling out to each other with love? Every stone, every grain of sand, every star is praying for reunion. The circle of each day, each season, each unimaginable kalpa returns us to each other.

Every prayer, even the smallest and most banal of petitions, sets our souls back on the path of the heart. We call out to our mothers, and reality rearranges itself to offer us intimate miracles and unexpected blessings. Sometimes, too, our prayers lead us into the depths, beyond the horizon, and to places so strange and unfamiliar that we are unnerved and terrified. We are calling out to our mothers and they are calling out to us, and we cannot know where we will reunite. How does the star feel as it moves closer to the black hole? How does the sand feel under the weight of the ocean? What is it like to leave behind all that is familiar and routine and seemingly safe? We cannot know where prayer will take us or imagine how prayer will change us; we can only trust that our mothers love us, have always loved us, and long to hold us in their arms again. We must put our faith in their love.

Empires rise and fall. Species come and go. A cosmos collapses and another world is born. And amid the cataclysms and catastrophes, the birth pangs and the cries of the infant, are the very transformations and reunions for which our souls have prayed.

At the start of the universe there was a vibration according to the scientists, a sacred sound according to the mystics, the first note of a new song. *Om* emerges from the nothingness. *Om, Om, Om.* But this first sound is an answer to an older sound still. Before this beginning souls called out to their mothers. *Ma, Ma, Ma.* Deep calls to deep. Heart calls to heart. The beginning is the answer to the end.

The mothers always answer with the wonder of creation, the miracle of life, the blessings of bodies. At the beginning is always the cry of a child and the love of a mother. We are the mothers who hear your cries.

The moment you begin to cry from the depths of your necessity and desire you will know that this is true.

## Chapter Eight

# THE LIES WE TELL OURSELVES

Once when Clark and I were down in Tennessee for a family reunion organized by his mother, we stopped at a local pharmacy to pick up a prescription for someone—his grandmother or his aunt, I can't remember. While we waited, I browsed the aisles of the little store in this remote mountaintop village and noticed giant bottles of vanilla extract on a bottom shelf. They were the size of magnums of champagne.

"I guess the women around here do a lot of baking," I said to Clark, confused. "I mean, I do a lot of baking, but I wouldn't use that much vanilla even if I were making cakes professionally."

Clark laughed. "We're in a dry county."

"What does that have to do with anything?" I asked.

"There are a lot of old ladies around here who don't drink. But they do have their afternoon cordial for their nerves."

"They *drink* the vanilla?" I was astounded.

"Like it's sherry, only it's as strong as bourbon," explained Clark. "But it's sold in a pharmacy, so it's medicinal. And it's just vanilla."

"It's 70 proof!" I exclaimed, looking at the tiny information on the enormous bottle.

"Exactly," said Clark.

We laughed about this for weeks at the expense of these old women who were drinking without having to acknowledge that they were drunks.

But my own mother engaged in a similar, much less humorous self-deception about her alcoholism. Five o'clock came, and it was respectable to have a drink—bourbon on the rocks, a tumbler full, the good stuff of course. Maybe a second glass if it had been a rough day. There was always wine with a fancy label at dinner, a bottle with a provenance that could be discussed with erudition. A second glass. A second bottle. By the end of her life she was buying big liters of cheap Jim Beam at the liquor store the next town over. She kept herself to two glasses, but the glasses got bigger and bigger.

"The *New York Times* had the most fascinating article about red wine," my mother would reliably announce to explain her inebriation. "It's about the French paradox. They can eat so much butter and red meat because a glass of red wine keeps their veins clear of cholesterol. Red wine is good for your heart."

Over the years the amount that was "good for the heart" varied. "How much was that again?" Clark would sometimes bait her at the end of a long, boozy meal.

"A drink before dinner is good for you," my mother would announce defiantly, her eyes narrowing. She could always tell when she was in danger of being mocked. "And a few glasses of wine are very important for your heart health. That's why the French are so healthy: because of all the wine they drink."

Only of course the whole study was bogus, promoted by a so-called journalist who had his own red wine problem. The real reason the French didn't die so much from heart attacks was because they had socialized medicine and better preventative care than Americans. But the *New York Times* was my mother's holy scripture and allowed her, as surely as those old ladies in Tennessee, the cloak of respectable convention to hide what was, in truth, a problematic addiction. My mother told herself, and me, that real addicts were drunks like my friend's mother Rita who drank straight vodka in the morning. Real addicts lost their jobs, got into trouble with the law, and couldn't function during the day. My mother could never admit that what she'd really lost to alcohol was herself—the creative, powerful woman of my earliest childhood.

As the night wore on and her glass was refilled, she oscillated between self-pity, resentment, and belligerence.

"My therapist told me not to marry your father after all, but I didn't listen to her and I ruined my life. It's all his goddamn fault. You're not going over there, are you, to see him?"

"Nobody understands me. I'm alone, always alone . . . the rest of you think you are so smart, so important, but you don't know anything, do you? Nothing." She'd blow through her lips derisively.

"You're just like your father. You think you're so special, don't you?"

I wanted her to sober up because I wanted to be intimate with her. Drunken conversations with her—and by the time I was in my twenties all our conversations were drunken conversations—were minefields of regret and fury. She often called me by my father's name as if he were the only person she was really speaking to anymore.

In the early days of her dementia, I thought it would make a difference if she stopped drinking. It might have—it's hard to know. I convinced my brother to talk with her because she allowed him a certain authority as a man she did not afford me. Like so many women, she trusted men more than women. He told me their conversation went really well—which it probably did, except that she called me up a few minutes later to berate me for trying to control her life.

"I know you were behind that phone call. These are all your machinations. You think I'm no good, don't you? What do you know about anything?" she hissed, before hanging up the phone.

In retrospect she was actually right.

Just like she pointed the finger at my friend's mother—"Now that's a real addict"—I pointed my finger at her. My problem was *her* drinking—not my own addiction.

Even as a teenager I knew I had a problem with sugar, and for a long time I blamed my mother for this. She'd given me those bowls of brown sugar lumps as a toddler; she'd stocked the pantry with cookies and candies;

she'd left frozen coffee cakes for me to heat up and eat whole when she had to be out of the house for one of her events. After my father left and I stopped eating, she was the one who made caramelized bread puddings to activate my appetite. I learned to keep myself thin by only eating sugar—oversweetened tea for breakfast, a Coca-Cola and a candy bar at the end of the day, a sticky cookie stuffed with chocolate chips and another and another and another.

"You buy a lot of cookies," the teenage clerk at the local bakery said to me one day in college.

I had been caught red-handed. I was exposed and ashamed. I stopped going to that bakery as certainly as my mother had stopped going to the local liquor store and drove to the nearest city to get her Jim Beam. I was slender in those days because all I ate was those cookies. I wasn't anorexic, I told myself, not like my sophomore year roommate who had to drop out for treatment. I wasn't bulimic, although sometimes I wished I could be. I just had a sweet tooth—an insatiable, inconsolable, ravenous need for sugar. Nothing was ever too sweet for me. When I waitressed in the summers, I'd end the evening with a bowl of Moose Tracks ice cream slathered in butterscotch and hot fudge, which I ate at home, alone, in a disassociated state of indulgence, desire, and self-disgust.

When I became a mother, my biggest challenge was having to pretend to eat like a normal person—regular meals, healthy snacks, protein, and vegetables—and manage the ever-increasing urgency of my dependence on the white stuff. I was so tired and overwhelmed, so alone and scared, and a little treat had always consoled me over the years. Let's make gingerbread men! Let's make brownies! Let's bake a cake. Of course, I'd finish everything off when the kids were asleep or at school. Between pregnancies, nursing, stress, and sleeplessness, I predictably began to put on weight, which made me feel more ashamed and stressed and in need of more of the sweetness I did not feel that life was offering me. Then, of course, I was always on a diet. My observant children noticed all of this.

There are so many different definitions of an addict—and they usually involve someone else's behavior and not our own. *I can hold down a job. I'm not doing anything illegal. I don't have a problem with gambling or shopping or eating or porn.* We invent all kinds of gradations and subtleties about the ways in which we habitually hurt ourselves, just so we can define ourselves as something other than what we know, deep down, we really are. How can we tell when we are in trouble?

I prayed for solutions to the addiction that did not address the addiction. I needed to lose weight. I needed to eat healthy. I needed to change my relationship to food and seeking "nourishment." I needed some quick fix that would readjust my metabolism. I tried so many different diets over the years—one in which chicken breasts and vegetables were boiled in vinegar, one in which I counted out almonds every night until I just started grabbing handfuls from the bag. I tried Adkins, South Beach, paleo, keto, and finally, broken-down hopelessness in a twelve-step meeting room for overeaters. Even then I knew that overeating wasn't the problem. Sugar was the problem, and what I really wanted was to be able to eat sugar and remain thin so nobody would be able to tell that I had a problem. I didn't want to get sober; I wanted to be a functional addict. Sugar turned me into a liar, wrapping myself in lies that always demanded a web of even more lies.

As an addiction, sugar is a much more recent problem than alcohol. Until the modern age, honey and maple syrup, and especially refined cane sugar, were luxury items primarily reserved for feast days and celebrations. There just wasn't a lot of them around. But the first crop that Columbus planted on Hispaniola was sugarcane. The crop thrived in the warm, wet climate, although its backbreaking production and harvesting necessitated an enormous ever-expanding labor force. Almost immediately, Columbus began enslaving the local population, and then captured individuals, into the production of sugar. So entwined was Western Hemisphere slavery with sugar that rumors spread that the bones of enslaved people were used in the processing to make sugar white. Even today, the sugar industry accounts for horrific violence against its indentured workforce.

Large-scale agriculture has always depended upon slavery since its inception, and its rewards have never really benefited anyone other than those at the top of its hierarchies. From the beginning, most workers would flee the toil of the fields for the ease of the hunter-gatherer lifestyle, just as they did in the newly colonized world. But in addition to ever-prevalent violence, the rewards of addictive substances kept them harnessed to the plow. The beer at the end of the day, the doughnut box for the coffee break, the little pill to take away the pain coerced obedience and suppressed revolution. With the rise of industrialization, sugar—refined cane sugar, corn syrup—became an insidious way of keeping people toiling in factories.

The very foundation of empire is addiction—to alcohol, to cigarettes, to pain relief, to gambling, to shopping, to hoarding, to accumulating, to demanding more and more. We—citizens of the city-state, the nation, the patriarchal empires—are hopeless before our addictions, committed to murder, war, ecocide, and suicide. We have become so deranged, and the natural world has been so depleted, that it can be impossible to even imagine another way of life. We cannot flee to some Edenic hunter-gatherer lifestyle in a world where the great forests have been felled, the streams no longer run with salmon, and the skies are empty of birds. We are in the middle of the sixth extinction of all life on Earth because we as a species are ravenous for more and more and more. Have we hit rock bottom yet?

Growing up, I used to hear that question a lot when people were talking about my friend's mother Rita. She was a beautiful, accomplished woman who'd had a successful career as a physical therapist before motherhood. She had a great sense of humor, a wealth of knowledge about books, and tremendous warmth. But she was nevertheless powerless before her addiction. "When she hits rock bottom, she'll sober up," I'd hear one of the adults whispering to another. My mother would shake her head and sigh, taking a drag on her cigarette. *What was rock bottom?* I wondered. Rita was suicidal and despondent. Eventually, I discovered that rock bottom, for a lot of people, was death itself. Rita died alone in a tenement apartment filled with broken vodka bottles, her esophagus having burst from so much drunken vomiting. She was in her early fifties. I was heartbroken at her funeral. I had liked her so much. How could someone with such gifts have committed to such a devastating path?

Yet is our species any different? Will we sober up from civilization before we hit rock bottom or eventually go extinct, taking the whole planet down with us?

In her short story "The Ones Who Walk Away from Omelas" the great science fiction writer Ursula K. Le Guin describes a city that is a visionary utopia—egalitarian, cultured, and peaceful. Everyone gets along. Everyone is happy and productive. The arts flourish. Life is beautiful. The laws work and are just. This is civilization, perfected at last. The only small problem is that in a dungeon deep underground a small child is imprisoned in filth and misery. To remove that child from suffering would mean the end of the magnificent achievements of Omelas. It's terrible, but it's only one child after all.

So most of the citizens simply ignore this harsh reality hidden somewhere beneath their finely paved streets. Others visit the child from time to time and feel better about themselves for having recognized that sometimes sacrifices must be made for the betterment of all. They shake their heads, marveling at their own compassion. Some people, however, can tolerate none of it—neither the degradation of the child nor the illusions of Omelas. They are the ones who walk away from it all.

As civilized human beings we all have that unmothered child hidden deep within us. Should we ever, after ten thousand years of tinkering, finally get civilization right, there would still be, beneath the foundation, absolute abjection.

We cannot tinker with civilization and get it right. No elected leader, no progressive program, no righteous nation or worthy cause, no set of laws or amendments, and certainly no religious agenda or technological solution will ever address the profound crisis we have created for ourselves. From almost the very beginning, civilization has been inventing and reinventing new rules and commandments to solve its problems—but the problems just get worse and worse and worse.

My life in my fifties looked happy and productive. I was selling books and teaching workshops. My grown children were navigating the ups and downs of adulthood with poise and imagination. My house was beautiful; my pets were thriving; my marriage was a blessing. But my stomach always hurt—from stress, from sugar, from shame about my reliance on sugar.

One terrible day I found myself in the emergency room with a tube threaded down my nose into my stomach, poking into my small intestine to try and force it open. I had a life-threatening bowel obstruction. The pain, even with morphine, was the worst I had ever known, so much worse than even childbirth. The tube was creating a rhythmic sucking which the doctors hoped, along with fasting, might invite my gut to relax. One theory was that scar tissue from gallbladder surgery decades earlier had strangled my intestines, but whatever the origin story, I knew that I had brought this on myself.

The ordeal had begun while I was working, resentfully, on a lucrative book doctoring project. The author, who was also deep into the divine feminine, was struggling with her writing. More than editing her ideas, I wanted to challenge them with my own. After all, my husband and I had written a book together about ancient devotions to the Great Mother, but our book tour had been cut short by COVID, and I was worried that it was not going to find its audience. We needed the money. I took the job. I compulsively chewed pistachios and corn chips while I reorganized the other author's manuscript. I was upset in ten thousand different directions, and all of my anger was going into crunching these hard salty foods. When the dyspeptic pain began, I assumed it was because I was just so angry about the editing I was doing and about the writing of my own I was neglecting, and, well, about everything.

Lying in my hospital bed, waves of agony coursed down through my throat into my belly. I shut my eyes, keeping as still as possible. In my head I said over and over again the syllables of the Hail Mary, a Christian prayer that had been my grandmother's daily devotion but which my husband Clark and I had discovered led back, grandmother by grandmother, to women who had been devoted not to a patriarchal god but the triple goddess of our ancestors—the maiden, the mother, and the crone.

*Hail Maiden full of graces*
*Thy beloveds are with thee*
*Blessed art thou among Mothers*
*And blessed is the fruit of thy womb: all life.*
*Holy Crone, Queen of the Cosmos,*
*Pray for us now and at the hour of our death.*

Was I going to die? Was this the final verdict on my compulsive overeating? Was my grandmother from the other side shaking her head at my gluttony? Was my mother sighing that I did not have enough vanity to manage my pleasures? The heart monitor beeped, and I opened my eyes in the darkened hospital room and looked out through the window at the night sky. The full moon was rising over the trees.

It was only then that I remembered, with a bottomless terror, that my own mother had died of a small bowel obstruction on the night of a full moon.

What was it I couldn't digest? If I got through this, I told myself, I would figure out how to eat; I would sober up from sugar, dammit, once and for all. I was bargaining with the cosmos. I wanted to be a wise old lady, a crone, and a grandmother. *Please,* I whispered to all of the mothers and grandmothers who had ever been, *guide me back to the land of the living.* At that moment out of the corner of my left eye I saw, as clearly as the moon itself, a black-winged being fall from the heavens right into the hospital room. A dark angel? A demon? A bird? A feathered messenger. But I didn't really know what the message was . . . was it a prophecy, a blessing, or a curse?

Somehow, I already understood that this was a message from my mother beyond the grave—one that she sent with her own death and that it would take me almost two decades to receive. She could have died from so many different things—from a fall, from her failing heart, from a stroke, from the cancer come back, from the pneumonia she kept catching, but instead, she died of a bowel obstruction. Perhaps nothing in the universe is random. Time, the physicists tell us, is not linear but folded over itself like a piece of paper made smaller to fit inside an envelope of reality. Had my mother, in the liminal realms of dementia, seen her daughter's future and found a way to send her a warning? You, too, will die this way, and I will be with you when you pass. Was I going to die?

Toward morning I began to feel movement within my body, air making its way from one end to another, the utter relief of passing gas. The tube was taken out. I moved on from broth and popsicles to applesauce and pureed vegetables. I was cleared a few days later to go on vacation with my family down to Cape Cod, the sand-strewn lands of my grandmother. We'd rented a small house near the seashore, and our first night there we all walked down to the beach. The waves lapped at the shore as the tide came in. The sun was setting into the ocean. A black bird dropped out of the sky into the water—just as I had seen in my hospital room.

"What was that?" I gasped.

"A cormorant," said Clark. "They fish at this time of the day."

Why had I never noticed these birds before? Why had one visited me as an apparition in the hospital? Googling them on my phone right there on the beach, I quickly discovered that they were used for hunting in Japan. A metal band was fastened around their necks, constricting their throats so that they could not swallow the fish they caught for their captors. Because of this, cormorants became associated in Japanese Buddhism with the figure of the hungry ghost—always eating and never satisfied.

Yet before they were enslaved by human beings, these elegant birds shared a different message—about the depths to which we needed to dive in order to find the answers to our problems. The healing I needed was deeper, older, and more mysterious than yet another diet or self-improvement plan. It was bigger and stranger than simply making peace with my mother's passions or my grandmother's devotions. How was I supposed to remove the scar tissue in my body, the constraints around my throat and voice, the thorns around my heart and its wildest yearnings? What was it I really wanted? A cormorant can plunge over a hundred feet beneath the surface of the ocean to find the treasure that it seeks.

I needed to dive deep into the depths of time, the depths of my own soul, to call forth the guidance not just of my mother and my grandmother but an entire ocean of ancestral mothers and grandmothers. Only they could help me get sober.

A year later I still binged on honey, lying to myself that it was healthier than the processed stuff, and collapsed in an episode of fainting and vomiting that had me rushed, again, to the emergency room. As soon as they determined I wasn't having a stroke or a heart attack, they stuck me in a back room covered in throw-up, like just another drunk they were trying to dry out. Really.

"I think she ate something that was no good for her," said the doctor to Clark and Sophie when the results came back.

That was certainly true.

Was that my rock bottom?

It was more like a crossroads in the middle of a thick forest. All around me was darkness. I could stay stuck where I was, surrendering to my compulsions, my blood sugar higher every year, risking cancer or dementia, or I could step off the path I had been on for so long and head into the mystery.

Addiction was familiar—sobriety was not.

I'd always told myself: lose weight and then you can have the cheese Danish or the chocolate bars or the cakes. But what if I said no to all of that forever? I could feel paths before me that I wanted to explore, books I wanted to write, adventures I still wanted to have, and most of all, grandchildren I wanted to hold in my lap. Like my mother, I knew I wanted them more than anything—but I did not want to be already dying, sick and incapacitated, when they arrived. I wanted playful, memorable time with them, and my children weren't even dating anyone serious yet.

On the way home I googled the patron saint of hopeless causes even though I already knew it was St. Jude. *Did people ever call on him for help getting sober?* I wondered. *Could he take time off from helping kids with cancer or was this an imposition for someone as busy as he most certainly was?* I looked down at my phone, surprised to see another name had come up next to his. There was another saint for the desperate and the hopeless: St. Rita. Pictures popped up, all the same, showing a woman dressed as a nun carrying an enormous cross on her back. I recoiled. I remembered my friend's mother Rita in her TV room, sprawled on the couch, out to lunch, maudlin and pathetic. I couldn't call on Rita. She'd died of her addiction. She never got better.

But what I had discovered in working with the dead—what I had in fact written a whole book about—was that often our very failures in life become our superpowers when we're on the other side of the veil. My father who had disinherited me in life was now generous beyond measure in death: when I reached out to him, I received a royalty check in the mail, more sign-ups for a workshop, an unexpectedly forgiven debt. Similarly, I had seen with my students over the years how the self-involved grandmother was now helpful or the sickly uncle was the healer at last. The teen who'd committed suicide knew exactly how to protect others from their despair. I felt bile rising in my throat as my stomach roiled. I had to admit to myself that I was secretly terrified that I might die like Rita, my own esophagus ruined because of endless reflux caused by my addiction.

I needed Rita to protect me from her fate. Rita never met her grandchildren, but I wanted to know mine.

That night I read about St. Rita. She had been a housewife in Cascia, Italy, in the fourteenth century. A victim of domestic violence, she is often depicted with a bleeding wound at the center of her forehead, explained away by the Church as a stigmata but more likely an injury that her abusive husband had inflicted. Eventually Rita's husband died, her violent sons died, and she found peace at last in a convent where she tended the honeybees.

"I can't even do honey," I said out loud, the Wikipedia page open on my phone glowing bright.

*But you need sweetness even so,* I heard St. Rita answer in my imagination. *Your whole life you have longed for sweetness; we all have in truth. It is that primordial sweetness that flows from your mothers' breasts, that flows from the stars themselves, the Milky Way, that I can help you experience again. I have been waiting for you to ask for my help for a long time.*

Alone in the dark, I began to cry. I looked up one of St. Rita's traditional prayers online and began memorizing it. I promised the Rita I had known that I would visit her grave if she helped me sober up, really sober up: No sugar. No honey. No maple syrup. Ever again. Not in this life. I wanted to be honest with myself. I didn't want to outsource my intuition, and I couldn't if I wanted to get sober. To strengthen my resolve, I voiced my determination out loud at my regular online prayer circle the next night. Immediately another woman in the group messaged me. "I resolved yesterday to sober up from sugar. This is my second day. You want to help each other do this? Keep each other on track?"

Neither of us fussed with diets or nutritional programs. We didn't tell each other what we ate. Our honesty with ourselves was our own business. But we checked in with each other at the beginning and end of every day, and we reached out when we felt our commitment wavering. The first days and weeks were brutal, and we messaged each other all the time. I prayed to Rita and St. Rita all day long. When I thought I might just give up, I thought about my friend and what it would mean to let her down, to leave her alone before her own addiction. My sobriety wasn't only for me; it was also for my friend. If addiction isolates us, sobriety begins to bring us back into relationship with others.

Because sugar is such a ubiquitous addiction, people were always trying to tempt me. Just one bite! Not even birthday cake? My resolve was strengthened by every sober alcoholic I had ever met who put their hand over their wineglass at the dinner table. If they could do it, I could do it too. My definition of sobriety was finally simple: no sugar. No date sugar, no coconut sugar, no maple syrup, no honey, no corn syrup, no unrefined cane sugar—and nothing with any of those substances in them. No sugar.

For a while, meat was my methadone. But eventually I began to discover that not only did I seem to have a different relationship to my own appetite, but my taste buds were slowly reviving. I began discovering whole new worlds of food and cooking I'd never enjoyed before. My cooking repertoire expanded even as I had to give up my identity as the family baker. Traditional meals needed to be reimagined. Still, I really looked forward to those meals for the very first time. I didn't lose weight, but that wasn't the point. It wasn't about how I appeared, but how I thought and felt.

Without the cacophony of self-flagellation, I could not only hear myself think; I could hear the whole world speaking more clearly. I felt more centered in my intuitions, as if my third eye was beginning to open like St. Rita's open eye at the center of her forehead. As my cravings subsided—and they did—I began to feel lighter, too. My burdens of shame and worthlessness were lifting.

One night, a few months into my sobriety, I dreamed that my mother and I were having high tea with the queen of England. Tiered trays were elegantly packed with delectable cookies and cakes. There were scones, strawberry jam, a chocolate cake. We were at the palace. The furniture and plates were edged in gold. "I don't eat sugar," I rudely announced to the queen. "But I'll have a cup of black tea." I woke up, liberated, praying not just for sobriety today and the next day, not just for sobriety for the rest of my life, but sobriety in my every dream, sobriety in all my lifetimes to come.

Stories of addiction and recovery abound in our addicted culture—the drunk or the druggie who burns down their life but finally, from the ashes, emerges chastened and renewed. But so many of our addictions in modern life are not only invisible but utterly acceptable. Not only do they not destroy us; they seem to help us live within the stresses and dysfunctions of modern life. One person shops too much; another hoards junk; and still another must make more and more money, accumulate more and more power, buy another house, another car, another anything that might stifle the sounds of those faraway whimpers. We are glued to our screens, certainly, but more dangerously we are addicted to ourselves—our issues and problems, our successes and achievements, our relentless fun house of mirrors in which we are always looking at ourselves looking at ourselves. We are all lying to ourselves, each in our own particular way, as surely as those old ladies pouring vanilla into their crystal glasses on a golden afternoon. Later they will pass out again, alone, unable to talk to their daughters on the phone about what is really in their hearts, terrified to remember what is in their hearts.

Is this what we want?

How will we ever sober up from patriarchal empire itself? How do we sober up from empire when empire is everywhere? We can no longer escape into the wilderness because what little wilderness is left is so depleted it can barely support the remaining insects and birds. Plastics run through our veins. Perhaps that's why our only consolation, like the defeated addict, is the eventual overdose. We are telling ourselves so many stories of dystopic collapse, the walking dead, hellscapes of death and destruction. If we are going down, we are bringing the whole planet with us. We start another war, drop another bomb, fell another forest.

I drive my car to the grocery store. I earn money to pay for that car. Even if that car is electric, even if I recycle, even if I offset my carbon footprint, even if I dumpster dive and live off the grid, I am still utterly embedded in this patriarchal catastrophe hurtling toward collapse. Does my personal sobriety even matter amid such atrocities? What does sobriety from civilization itself really look like?

Maybe sobriety from empire is knowing how long it is going to take to get sober. Maybe it is knowing that the collapse of empire, terrifying as it is, will be a kind of answer to our prayers. Maybe we have to trust the long story of our souls—so much longer than a lifetime, a species, or an epoch—in order to find our way back to real sobriety.

My mother drank because she felt defeated by life. She'd lost her career, her marriage; nothing had gone the way she wanted, and she didn't trust herself to want anything anymore other than the consolations of grandchildren. She suppressed all of her yearning and her passion with alcohol. It all just hurt too much. I only know a little of Rita's story and nothing of those old women in Tennessee, but I suspect they were not much different. They could not imagine another life than the one they found themselves stuck inside.

But there is always another story. There is always another life.

The path of sobriety is dark and unknown when we are still addicted. As we begin to walk it, we have to trust our feet, feeling for stones and roots with our toes, moving slowly. Gradually our eyes begin to adjust, and the moon offers enough light for us to see a step or two ahead. We begin to notice the stars and accept their ancient guidance. An owl hoots, and we know we are not alone. We begin to know that the ground beneath our feet, the darkness that surrounds us in all directions, is filled with nothing but mothers and grandmothers who have loved us for lifetimes. They know how to see in the dark. They remember the long story of our souls. They can hold the big picture. They can guide us where we need to go.

Whatever marvels we constructed without these mothers were lies that did not sustain us, nourish us, or love us. The moment we begin to call to them, they begin to answer us with the sweetness we have truly craved.

What would it be like to live in a world where everyone knows that these mothers and grandmothers are real and are here? What would it be like to live in a world where everyone, without exception, feels mothered in the ten directions, by the living, by the dead, by kith and by kin, by plants and animals, by stones and stars, by all that is?

We cannot imagine such a world until we begin to walk toward it.

# A Message from the Mothers of Mystery

The stream rushing down the side of the mountain in the springtime accepts the shape-shifting of warmth and the urgency of gravity, pushing past rocks, rising over obstacles, longing for the wide waters of an ocean it remembers but can no longer envision. Those waters are different than the stream recalls. The ocean has experienced vast cycles of change—the beings that have reveled in its depths only to disappear, the expansions across the land, the retreats into ice. The stream, too, has gone through droughts and cataracts, become a mighty river, and meandered through the marshes. When the stream and the ocean are reunited, they will marvel at all they have known and become, and what they now can become together.

There is a story passed down from the ancients about a musician and his beloved that ends, predictably and as all short stories of single lives end, with a death and a departure. On the very night that Orpheus weds Eurydice a snake bites the bride. It feels particularly cruel and unfair. The young lover weeps and wails. He can call forth the songs of the trees and the stones, but he cannot sing his wife Eurydice back to life. The beauty of his keening touches the hearts of all beings in the unseen realms. "Oh Orpheus, Orpheus," we called out to him. "She is here with us. Come, come, know that she is here and will be with you again."

We were trying to help this lost young man understand the impossible mysteries of life and death, of departure and reunion, of the soul's epic journey through space and time.

But Orpheus did not understand. "I will cross the veil, the river, the line between life and death, whatever separates us from each other, and rescue her and bring her back to life. This I can do," he proclaimed with the audacity of youth.

"Of course you can do this," we said to him. "We love you and your songs. They bring the whole world back into bloom. We want the love between you and Eurydice to endure and regreen the Earth. Of course we do. But if you come here to bring her back to life, there is only one thing you must remember: you must not look back. As long as you do not look back, you will be reunited with your love."

The stream cannot look back. It cannot return to the quiet pools in the forest, frozen and still, as the snows fall all around it. It cannot become again a shallow burble in the mossy shadows where the frogs and salamanders play. It can only follow gravity down, down, down. It is no different with time, which is always moving onward, onward, onward.

We will never find what we desire by looking backward.

So many become stuck in an impossible nostalgia for a time that they have lost that has long since vanished and never really was. *If only we could get back to that still point of paradise,* they say, not knowing that Eden was never still, that all of nature and the whole cosmos are always on the move—changing, becoming, and transforming. Nature doesn't look back. One species goes extinct, and another flourishes in the ecological niche it has vacated. Continents collide and divide. Almost all life vanishes from the face of the Earth—and upon that blank slate the planet draws an entirely different vision of creation.

Eurydice will always return to Orpheus. Love stories have no beginning and no end. But Eurydice as Orpheus knew her is gone. Her body has returned to the earth, and her soul has found the body of another life. Can Orpheus find her as she is now, as who she has become? Will he recognize her as the dragonfly that follows him down the path, as the nightingale that sings to him in the moonlight, as the unexpected trillium blooming at the heart of the forest? Can his love for her become a love of all that she is becoming?

Let us tell a new story of Orpheus and Eurydice, reborn, returned to each other, recognizing each other's songs, falling in love again, married, dancing, laughing, eventually an old wrinkled couple holding hands, gazing into each other's eyes, knowing that even so they will have to part again and find each other again. Others look upon them, shaking their heads and wondering what these simple people could possibly have done to deserve such blessings.

We look back because that way is known to us and seemingly safe. Even the horrors and traumas, the disappointments and resentments are familiar. The way forward is unknown, unpredictable. When the stream returns to the ocean, the plesiosaurs have vanished but the whales are singing. The story of our souls before we were born into this life is mostly a mystery to us. What lies before us is also a mystery. We have no idea where we are or where we are going. Our way, the way of the mothers, is the way of mystery, and hidden inside those dark mysteries are unfathomable miracles.

The stream travels into the unknown without any other map than the gravity of love. Love is what carries us to an ocean of belonging. We heed the call of our desire and accept the guidance of our hearts.

You have called out to your ancestral mothers, and we have answered. We have never forgotten you, and we have sent into the future none of us can yet know all our love for you. But do not try to return to us; seek what we are becoming.

## Chapter Nine

# TALKING ABOUT REALITY

My mother had no conscious relationship to prayer, devotion, or any outward manifestations of a spiritual life. She didn't go to church, meditate, read self-help books, or have opinions on anything mystical or mysterious. She was a modern materialist who believed in facts, all the news that was fit to print, and something she called, in moments of extreme exasperation and fury, "reality."

"I'm talking about reality, Perdita!" she would announce at the height of some particularly terrible fight. She'd straighten her back and toss her head, defiantly speaking her truth. It was the trump card she played when she felt threatened or vulnerable. Her reality usually obliterated feelings, sensations, and, most definitely, any inchoate perceptions and intimations. Her reality felt like it obliterated *my* reality and all I experienced and wanted—a place where dreams were not just psychological mechanisms, imagination could carry us into possible futures, and the darkness held both mysteries and wonders. I was certain my reality was a place where my mother and I might find a lost experience of intimacy—and she saw it as nothing but an attack on everything she felt really mattered.

I remember her lambasting a cousin of mine one boozy night for daring to suggest that *Buffy the Vampire Slayer* was a truly great TV show. The cousin had a teenage daughter coming into her power, after all. "Oh, you are so full of shit," she said to this man who was trying to make polite dinner table conversation. "Buffy the fucking vampire slayer. That's what's the matter with young people today: They have no idea what's really going on. They aren't thinking about population expansion, nuclear proliferation, or the military-industrial complex. What do vampires have to do with *reality*?" She blew through her lips dismissively. "*Buffy the Vampire Slayer*—what a waste of time. *Pffft!*"

To say that her response was disproportionate to the topic at hand was an understatement. As the embarrassed guests poured themselves more wine or excused themselves to help out in the kitchen, my mother ranted and fumed. She was trying to express something with words she did not have, in a language she'd never learned, about the truth of her experience that no one seemed to get. Buffy and my poor cousin took the fall.

Young women didn't discover they could slay the vampires of patriarchy; they were defeated by them. That was the real story. That was my mother's reality.

I tried sometimes, ineptly, to suggest that there were other perspectives.

She came to visit me the autumn of my junior year in college when I was living in a ramshackle house with other students. She sat at our tiny kitchen table, clearly horrified by our squalor, not touching the terrible cup of coffee I'd made for her. She sighed, turning her face toward the sun while I extolled the genius of my favorite teacher.

"She's this brilliant Pakistani woman, and she's read everything, and she's so beautiful and wise. I feel like she's shifting my perspective about, well, everything, showing me how to step back and look at the invisible structures and assumptions that create our reality," I enthused.

My mother pursed her lips, irritated and also jealous. I began ranting about economies of money and power, and my mother sighed. "Do you think any of this will convince your father to send me his back alimony?" she laughed ruefully.

"But Mum," I insisted, "why let him control you that way? Go back to work! Move back to Boston! Fuck him! Find someone else."

"Oh, Perdita, what you don't know," she snapped, her rage simmering below the surface.

"You don't have to be a victim! Why do you always want to be a victim? Why don't you put your faith in something else?"

My mother's eyes narrowed. She drew her spine straight and squinted at me. "Faith?" she scoffed. "Are you depressed?"

I was twenty years old and trying to make sense of an onslaught of inexplicable perceptions—memories that did not fit into my timeline, dreams that predicted the future, the feeling that this one life was not the only life, not the only way. But I didn't dare confide in her about any of that. Instead, I said something about belief in the invisible world. "There are mystical realities beyond the material. I know it!" I insisted.

"*Pffft!*" she dismissed me. "One day you'll have to live in the real world."

I didn't understand until many years after she was gone what she was really talking about when she was talking about reality. She was right: there was so much I did not know. I didn't think about her driving four hours on the expressway by herself, one eye half-blind from polio, to come and see me regularly. I didn't think about how it felt to have her daughter flaunt the education that had been denied to her, just as the men close to her had always done. I could not understand what it felt like to have been born a mighty fertility goddess and transformed into a suburban housewife. She was talking about all the very real ways her dreams had been dashed, her desires extinguished, her relevance erased as she aged into invisibility. Her reality was a box with impermeable walls that trapped her in conventionality. She didn't see any way out.

"Isn't God part of reality?" I tried one last time.

"God?" she said, baffled, as if even the word itself were utterly meaningless. It wasn't that my mother didn't believe in God, but rather that the whole topic of belief or disbelief was in itself profoundly immaterial to her.

Looking back, I wish I could have simply summoned her long-gone mother to sit with us. I, too, no longer have any interest in an abstract deity, a monotheistic god, or even the very idea of gods and goddesses as special beings apart from our ancestors. I wish I could have asked if her mother and her grandmother were a part of her reality. I wish I could have summoned all of our mothers—not just the women, but the cats we loved, the roses she'd tended, the departed friends we'd shared. I wish I could have told my mother that I believed in her, that I would always believe in her, no matter if she were alive or dead, and that I knew she would drive to find me wherever I was, no matter what, and sit with me and listen to me, even if she thought I was full of shit.

I wish in that moment we could have experienced the mothering we both needed beyond each other, the mothering that would let us love each other without fear or resentment.

I wish I could have shown her that our ancestral mothers are the loophole in reality, that their reality is as embodied as the dirt, as fertile as the darkness, as magical as the dead. Every mother has a mother. It's mothers all the way down into the deepest depths of time. I wish my mother and I could have been time travelers together—because, of course, the person who taught me to time travel, without even knowing it, was my mother.

My mother loved history, which was for her less about the conquests of the great men than the outfits of the ordinary people. Our home was filled with books documenting everyday costumes through the ages—the hats people had worn, the shoes, the rising and falling hemlines, the expanding hoopskirts, the drape of cloth, the textures, the colors. "What goes around comes around," my mother always said. "The Romans were wearing bikinis, and the Minoans were going topless." When everyone was in a tizzy about men's long hair in the sixties, my mother kept reminding people that it was the Prussian army, precursors to the Nazis, who preferred the buzz cut. "Hair is an expression of personal identity, and fascist groups always want to homogenize appearances—this haircut, that kerchief. I say let people be whoever they want to be." Nevertheless, she dyed her own hair for years in order to look younger. We are all susceptible to cultural pressures.

Our house was filled with old costumes my mother had created for various productions. Putting them on changed how you felt about yourself.

A corset was a literal prison; an enormous hat made you feel taller, an ornate brocade robe more special. How people adorned themselves told you so much about who they were, how they thought about themselves, what mattered to them. This wasn't history as it was written down in the official records but as it was lived in a past moment in time. A costume was a magical way of summoning that direct experience. When I was Amy March in a production of *Little Women* at our local community theater as a teen, all of us actors would bump into each other when waiting backstage in the darkness, our hoopskirts colliding in a recreation of the enforced distancing of the Victorian era.

So much of acting, too, is a way of transcending one limited way of being and knowing who you were. That was what I loved most about being in theatrical productions—not just becoming someone else, but knowing that someone else existed within me. During the medieval revels and ancient feast days, people often took on other identities through costumes—men became women, women men; peasants wore the crowns of kings, and kings transformed into animals. Our Halloween celebrations are a meager remnant of what was once a powerful, seasonal reminder that we are all so much more than we appear to be. The beggar at your door might be an angel; the buck you hunted might once have been your child; the grandchild in your arms might once have been your grandmother. Each of our souls has known so many different incarnations, so many different lives and bodies.

As a child, I often had the feeling, derived from so many of the fantasy novels I'd read, that in the right moment and in the right frame of mind I might be able to step from one time into another, one body into another, one reality into another. I might be able to slip through the wardrobe door at any moment to a different realm. At dusk on a summer evening at the edge of the forest, I might enter a golden glade that became an entirely different world. It felt possible to me. If I could change my clothes, could I not shapeshift my very being as well?

My mother handed me a book to read when I was about twelve about a man who time traveled in just such a manner. I had never dared confide in her about my imaginative life, my elaborate daydreams, worried that she would think there was something the matter with me, something off, something crazy. She told me she was giving me *Time and Again* by Jack Finney because it was a "simply marvelous historical record of New York in the nineteenth century."

The novel was about a man who shifted his reality, not with a special spell or an elaborate machine, but simply by changing his state of mind. The premise of the book was that a top secret government organization had realized that if, as quantum mechanics posits, time is not linear but rather folded over itself like a piece of origami paper, then what keeps us inside of one experience of time rather than another is simply an elaborate matrix of cultural markers—the language we speak and think in, the sensory familiarities, the reference points like newspapers and cars and airplanes in the sky. Remove those markers or shift them, and time itself would become something else. In any place in the world, all time is present—just as it is in a rock on the side of the mountain that shows the striations, like a ream of paper, of layers and layers of epochs.

The main character undergoes an elaborate yet relatable reprogramming of his own place in history. He moves into a building not renovated since the nineteenth century. He begins wearing different clothes made from authentic fabrics. His food and newspapers and books, all historically accurate, are delivered to him by actors in period dress as well. Will he open the door one day and step into another era? Of course he will.

What I began to wonder, even as a teenager, was how often we were slipping through the paper folds of time without even realizing it. What if in our dreams, liberated from our waking certainties, we were able to access the experiences and memories of other lives? Wasn't this how a place could feel like two or three places at once, a person two or three different people we had known? As we emerge from sleep, we translate our adventures into the language of our current reality. The dreams we cannot hold on to, perhaps, are from lifetimes so foreign to our everyday experience that it is almost impossible to make sense of them upon awakening.

Forget outer space or the depths of the ocean: the great uncharted territory is the realm of sleep. Scientists don't even know what dreams really do—only that if we are deprived of them our lives fall to pieces. The problem, of course, as with most modern science, is fundamentalist notions of time and space, being and consciousness. The researchers were confused to discover that even in the womb before we have ever experienced a waking life, we are already dreaming. What could we possibly be dreaming *about*?

One scientist, Mark Blumberg, suspects that we are "learning how to have a body." For Blumberg this is mostly about biological mechanisms that he documents after implanting all manner of horrors into the heads of baby rats and watching how they twitch. Yet I think Blumberg is probably onto something he cannot spiritually comprehend. We are learning about the bodies we will have through the bodies we *have* had. We are remembering what it is like to have so many other different bodies: bodies that crawled and flew and swam, bodies that suffered and died, bodies that loved and lost and loved again, bodies whose experiences we can recover when we are asleep and can visit to reclaim what we need for these bodies we are currently inhabiting.

Or maybe we are always in many bodies simultaneously. When time is no longer linear, when it is folded over itself, then a soul, like an electron, can be in more than one place at once.

In my yoga class I take the shape of dogs and cows, eagles and trees, activating a somatic knowing I can barely articulate, much less understand. At night I feel my roots meander through the darkness of soil, my wings catch currents of air as canyons unfold beneath me, my tail guide me ever deeper into the depths. I awaken, remembering that I have this body but also that I have had many bodies and my soul contains them all.

The modern idea of time travel only emerges in our stories as we lose our sense of dream time and begin to live more and more narrowly within the rigid and relentless lines of linearity, evolution, and progress. The Bible posits a beginning to time and thus, ultimately, an end-time scenario that finds its ultimate expression in a theological assembly line that conveys us into the bin of heaven or the trash can of hell.

My obsession with time travel initially led to studying history in college, but I eventually switched to major in theater for the opportunity to truly immerse myself in other times and selves. At one of my first jobs in my twenties I was tasked with teaching "World Civilization" to high school students and found myself asking for the first time what civilization really was and what realities it had enforced. When I met Clark, who, disillusioned by both Christianity and Buddhism, was asking similar questions about various religious traditions, we began exploring together paleoanthropology and what we started to call the "belief-sphere" of our most ancient ancestors. I translated our research into writing a silly middle grades time travel series about a modern family hosting foreign exchange students that came not only from different countries but different eras as well—the boy from Greece was really from the city-state of Sparta, the Egyptian was from the age of the pharaohs. Much of the humor derived from the misunderstandings not just about food and hygiene but also completely different perceptions of animals, plants, and unseen realms. What had it been like to live in a world where everything—even stones, even rivers—was sentient and alive?

Around that time a friend of mine asked me if I was a fan of *Dr. Who.*

"Isn't that some cheesy old English television show?" My mother had actually watched it, and we had often teased her about how hokey it looked. Mostly we assumed it was part of her nostalgia for all things British, from strong black tea to *Country Life* magazine to anything having to do with the queen.

My friend's eyes widened. "You've never seen it? You have got to plunge in at once. It's been on the air for decades, and it's all about time travel. But start with the most recent episodes. It's the best."

The show has been able to perpetually reinvent itself over the years—with new actors and directors and writers—because the main character, the titular Doctor, is a "time lord" who can regenerate himself into new bodies while still retaining all of his old memories. This time lord, the last of his people, travels the cosmos to save planets from evil cyborgs who want their destruction. Clark and I were hooked almost instantly, especially since we both regarded the series as a metaphor for reincarnation and the need to recover the long story of our souls in order to meet the spiritual challenges of the sixth extinction. The more I explored the simultaneous rise of time travel literature with our commitment to industrialization at all costs, the more it seemed it was all about going back in time to find something we'd lost in the past to ensure that we would not disappear in the future.

*Dr. Who* was a constant reminder that our greatest resource was the recovery of a completely different experience of time. Rather than live within the relentless onslaught of linear time, we could recover again—in our dreams and our reveries—the mercies of circular dream time where nothing was lost and everything could be returned to us.

In a strange "timey-wimey" coincidence, *Dr. Who* premiered on November 23, 1963, the day after the assassination of John F. Kennedy. That world-shaking event overshadowed the simultaneous deaths of two writers: Aldous Huxley, the seer who wrote *Brave New World*, a book about our commitment to an artificial utopia that keeps us dependent on drugs and technology, and C. S. Lewis, who envisioned the ultimate dystopian nightmare in *That Hideous Strength*, in which a human head disconnected both from its body and the body of the world is utterly devoted to its own technology. As it sometimes does, time had collapsed on that November day, spawning a thousand conspiracy theories and no end of other time travel adventure narratives, including Stephen King's visionary tale *11/22/63* about nuclear apocalypse.

Was my mother aware of any of this? If I couldn't tell my mother about my dreams that took me to places where I one day arrived in real life or my reveries that offered visions of future events, perhaps she, too, had premonitions and memories that she spoke about to no one? How much did she sequester from her consciousness so as not to end up diagnosed and hospitalized like her mother?

On my daily hike up the mountain near my house there is a narrow stretch of path—steep and wooded, cascading in rocks to a cleft of streams and moss to my right—that I walked in dreams long before I moved to the Catskills. In those dreams, sometimes I am simply *there*—fully present in this place, immersed in my thoughts, and feeling everything deeply. I know exactly where I am, but not entirely *when* I am. Sometimes, I think I have walked on this path in different lands and in different times. I think I will always be walking on this path.

As I step down that narrow mountain path one spring afternoon, a salamander crawls into a patch of sunlight. Tomorrow the mountain laurel will begin to bloom. In the fall, the oak leaves will cover the forest floor. The stream will turn to ice. And then it will melt and freeze again. How does the water flowing out of the spring in the mountainside, water that fell from the clouds a million eons ago, experience time? How does the stream dream?

To feel the depth and width of time all around and within us is also to know how miracles happen—outside of the linear inevitabilities of cause and effect, outside of logical rational certainties. We pray to our ancestors, and we know our ancestors are us, here now, walking this path. We pray for our descendants, and we are praying for ourselves. Magic happens in the secret folds of time and space when one place is also another place, one time another time.

In time travel stories, the adventurers always go back to the past to rescue themselves.

How was I born knowing that worlds can end?

As surely as a day can be erased by a night of sleep, a life could be erased by death, an entire planet by extinction.

That I grew up hearing my parents talk about the imminent dangers of nuclear war, that an actual war that my older brother might have to fight in was raging on the television screen every night in the kitchen, that my mother took me as a child to see a Disney film about classical music that brought to vivid cartoon life the annihilation of the dinosaurs, showing the sky raining fire, devastation across the planet, the slow walk of despair as beast after beast succumbed to the terrors of a dead Earth—all was only confirmation of what I already knew, what I was born knowing: anything can die at any moment, and everything will die at some moment.

An astrologer once told me this was because so many of the planets were in the eighth house of death in my chart. But so many of my planets are in the eighth house of death because I was born remembering that worlds had died, that everyone I loved had died, that I had died—again and again and again.

My dreams from the time I was small were filled with cataclysms. I was in mountains somewhere—hiding, hunted, on the run from an enemy, an army. I was racing up a hill, while behind me a huge wall of water rose to engulf a village. I walked through a blasted wasteland, all life extinguished, the buildings in ruins, the birds, the insects, the animals, the vegetation, the people all vaporized in an instant. I woke up scanning the skies for planes, listening for the whistle of a bomb, waiting for the blinding whiteness of a nuclear blast.

It unnerved me that my nighttime visions often came true. I found myself walking on a road I had written about in my dream journal, meeting a man I already knew, stepping into a moment of déjà vu, synchronicity, eerie simultaneity. I had no way to make sense of any of this. When I brought my fears of nuclear devastation to a therapist, we spent much of our time talking about the cold war of my parents' marriage, a discussion which never touched the deep terrors within me. I threw myself into the nuclear freeze movement, marching and protesting, but feeling little relief when Gorbachev and Reagan signed the first de-escalation agreements. As a young teacher I decided that all of my one hundred tenth-grade students were going to enter a Japanese essay contest about the mistake of nuclear weapons. I had them reading the accounts of survivors and first responders. It all had very little to do with the curriculum, but the students began to share my obsession and, even though we were competing with young people all over the world, took all the top prizes. A Japanese journalist came to interview me because they had never had such an American response to the yearly event. I answered his questions very reasonably, discussing the military-industrial complex and never explaining that I had been haunted by images of nuclear war my whole life.

What is the past and what is the future in our dreams? When the past and future are folded over each other, how can one inform the other and guide our steps in the present?

One night soon after I met Clark, I dreamed I was inside of a nuclear missile just before it detonated in a city canyon, skyscrapers on every side. The missile was filled with people in orderly rows whose faces were lit from within, each of them holy and sacred. An older woman turned and whispered to me a prayer that was on her lips. I awoke with it on mine. I didn't know what to do with this dream except to say this prayer, this mantra, over and over again, until it was part of my heartbeat.

Over the next few years, I found myself saying this prayer when I was washing the dishes, driving the car, or digging in the garden. It became such a part of my morning run that certain syllables became connected to particular trees. "Three more mantras and I'll be up the hill," I'd know as I huffed and puffed along the road. Lying in bed, feeling my heartbeat, I felt the words of the prayer. I began to offer the prayer to each of the dead. I would say the name aloud of someone on the other side, then utter the syllables of the mantra.

The years passed and the kids were now going to the local elementary school down the road. I was writing plays for a local children's theater company and working for an educational publisher. One morning I sat down at my computer to begin the day's tasks when I saw a small headline on AOL. A plane had just flown into a building in Manhattan. "How terrible," I thought, imagining the crash of a small prop plane into a skyscraper.

"Perdita, come quick," yelled Clark from downstairs. He'd turned on the television after seeing the headline himself, and together we watched as the second jet threaded through the skyscrapers of New York City and roared into the Twin Towers.

"Oh my god, oh my god," wept Clark.

"There are people on that plane," I realized with total horror.

"Of course there are people on that plane," cried Clark. "And in the buildings too."

"But I know those people. Those are the people . . ."

Stunned, Clark simply stared at me.

"It wasn't a nuclear missile. It was a plane." I was so upset I thought I might vomit. How could it be? I had seen those passengers sitting in rows, knowing that they were inside an airplane turned into a bomb, and yet . . . and yet . . . Tears were streaming down my face.

"What are you talking about? People are dying!"

"My dream."

On the television screen the towers were on fire; people were jumping to their deaths. We watched as the towers collapsed, shaking, holding each other. Finally, I couldn't take it anymore. I fled the house and ran down to the pond in our backyard. I needed to find some way to make sense of what was happening. I sat down beside a patch of milkweed pods just beginning to open, and Clark came down and sat beside me.

"I saw them years ago in my dream. . . . I don't know how to explain it . . ."

"Maybe you were praying for them?" Clark suggested quietly.

"No," I knew. "It's like a fairy tale. I don't understand it. I don't have words for any of it. I can't explain it."

Clark laid his hand over mine. The sky above us was so blue, the air crisp and clear. How could the day be so beautiful and filled with such terror and violence? Something dark and wet was unfolding on a green milkweed leaf. A butterfly was emerging from a camouflaged cocoon. It turned itself toward the sun, opening its brittle wings fully as it did so. We picked up the kids at school, and all day long we moved between the nightmare unfolding on the television screen and the simple beauty of the monarch learning to use its wings down by the pond.

In the years following, many people would share their premonitions about this catastrophic event. A friend would show us the paintings his mother had done just before she died in the early eighties, all showing that iconic scene of people covered in ash fleeing the falling debris. I began to discover how common it is for people to see calamities before they happen. One British psychologist documented how, in the days leading up to the Aberfan mine collapse that buried an entire elementary school in 1966, not only had many of the children woken their parents to tell them about terrifying nightmares of death and destruction but people all around the country had visions of what was about to occur.

In his fascinating book *Time Loops*, the journalist Eric Wargo documents many such premonitions, positing that we are sending ourselves "memories from the future" to guide our present realities. While this may certainly be true, it doesn't tackle something more mysterious about those visions and perceptions that don't even involve us. If there is nothing we can do to prevent a calamity, why are we seeing it? Why was my friend's mother obsessed with an event that would happen after she was dead? There is something, finally, almost too utilitarian and individualized about Wargo's hypothesis, intrigued by it as I was. Why was I in that plane just before it hit the World

Trade Center? Why did I receive that prayer from that woman? Why did it so effortlessly become part of my heart?

It was in addressing someone else's concerns that I found the answer to my own. I was at a weekend workshop on activating inner psychic resources when a middle-aged woman in the audience spoke up, visibly distressed. "I *am* psychic," she said, her voice rising in hysteria, "but I don't know what to do about it. I see car and plane crashes before they happen to people I don't even know. Who do I contact? What do I do with this information? It torments me! Every night I fall asleep, terrified about what might unfold and how helpless I'll feel."

The workshop presenter nodded with genuine concern but fell back, unfortunately, on a psychological interpretation. "You should ask yourself what these dreams have to do with your own life. They are offering you information. What is it?"

The woman, running her hands through her disheveled hair, looked like she couldn't breathe. "I've done that for years," she muttered. Her face reddened. She was about to burst into tears. "But these events have *nothing* to do with me."

It felt like I was looking in a mirror. Wasn't that the real question that had brought me to this workshop, the one I was too terrified to ask? I felt the urgent need to relieve this woman's evident suffering—but the only way to do that was to make sense of what was happening to her and to me.

Some years earlier I had met the psychic Julie Ryan, a businesswoman who, after the death of her mother, began "knowing" when people were close to death. Her life was transformed by her experience helping others prepare for the transitions of their loved ones. She explained to me how those on the other side gathered close to the departing soul, ready to welcome them home. But when their mothers appeared—their biological mother, their adopted mother, their grandmothers, their foster mother, the person who had raised them—then they were ready to let go of one life and prepare for another. Our mothers are waiting for us on the other side. No one dies alone.

All our mothers from all our lifetimes are waiting for our inevitable reunion.

I remembered once coming up from a subway station into the city to find myself in the middle of an emergency. A man who appeared to be homeless, his cup in front of him, his garbage bags strewn around him, was dying. Police and emergency workers were trying to revive him. From only a few feet away, I watched him take his last breath, his eyes on me as he passed. I prayed for him. I didn't know what else to do. I invited him to join my ancestors without ever knowing his name.

Perhaps in one lifetime or another he was my child and I arrived as one of his mothers beside him as he crossed over. Was it any different when I came upon a deer or possum taking their last breaths on the side of the road after being hit by a car? What of the nurses who were often the only person with someone as they drew their last breath? Surely it was no coincidence. They were mothers helping children from lives they did not remember cross over. Our mothers are always there with us on both sides of the veil.

During a break in the workshop, I went over to the woman who had asked the question about her prophetic visions. She was standing outside looking at the trees.

"Excuse me," I interrupted her reveries. "But I also see terrible things that I can't do anything about."

"You do?" She turned, startled. "Why?"

I think I finally knew. "Those people you see? In car accidents and plane crashes? They are calling out for their mothers—and you hear them in your dreams and show up to be with them. They need you as they are dying. They need their mothers with them at that moment, and you are one of those mothers. You are a mother who hears their cries."

She was speechless, staring at me, wide-eyed. Slowly, she began to nod. "That's what everyone in my family calls me: Big Mama."

"How old are your children?" I asked.

"I don't have any children," she answered. "Which is why it's funny that's what everyone calls me. I think it's because I cook for everyone."

"You show up," I said. "You're a big mama out there in the world. We all have so many children if only we could remember."

She nodded, taking it all in. "But what do I *do*?" she asked at last.

"You are already doing it," I told her. "Just claim who you really are."

Before I met Clark in my thirties, I wasn't sure I would become a mother. I didn't feel up to single parenthood either practically or emotionally. I was living in New York City at the time, besieged daily by the suffering I saw all around me—not just the addiction and the poverty but the sheer concrete assault of urban life on meaning and joy. I was looking out the window of a high-rise one day across the grid of streets and avenues teeming with too many people, when I realized that it didn't matter whether I had children or not. I could still be a mother. Mothers were needed here more than ever. What if everyone in this city were my child from some other life? I didn't need some particular biological experience to be a mother. I needed a different state of mind.

The image of the mother that patriarchy has cultivated as surely as a genetically modified crop—resistant to pests and drought, chemically toxic, and lacking in essential nutrients—is selfless, sentimental, and unattainable. That idealized mother is the womb with no desire, the giver who needs nothing, the suppliant, the slave, and ultimately the scapegoat. She is also, most importantly, isolated and alone. Whether she is a tradwife making her own sourdough bread or a harried executive rushing the kids to day care, she never has enough hands, enough time, enough help. She is always failing. She has been engineered to fail so that the blame for all of our patriarchal problems can be laid at her feet.

But what if our presidents and leaders remembered that they were mothers not of these people or those people but all peoples, all beings? What if our generals and soldiers saw themselves as mothers of every soul on the other side? What if our prison guards and police officers knew they were the mothers of all those behind bars? What if our CEOs and CFOs knew they were the mothers of trees, of birds, of bees, of fish, of rare minerals hidden in the womb of the Earth? Would we even need or want politicians and armies and corporations anymore?

What if it were each of our callings to recover the memories of ourselves as mothers? What if boys became men when they became mothers? What if everyone in our circles were motherly? What if there weren't one beleaguered mother to meet all of our needs—either human or divine—but a world filled with mothers who have always loved us?

To imagine such a world feels, at this dire moment of end-stage empires battling to the death of the planet, like a ridiculous, maybe even dangerous, daydream. But to recover the memories of ourselves as mothers is to know that we have seen the world collapse countless times before and have shown up to hold all our children as they transitioned through the ending. We do not turn away from the agonies and the sorrows. We are the ones easing others back into the dark womb of the cosmos. We know that those wombs are fertile, creative, and desirous of life. To recover the memories of ourselves as mothers is to give birth to joys beyond measure and miracles beyond imagination. To recover the memories of ourselves as mothers is to feel joined in this work by all that is—by every flower, every cloud filled with rain, every birdsong at the end of the day, by the stars above and the very stones beneath our feet. The mother is not an individual identity but a collective reality.

I have been mothered by my mother's body. I have been mothered by teachers, by friends, by men, by the old and by children, by strangers I have met by chance. I have been mothered by hemlocks and maples and oaks, by the mountain behind my house, by the Earth, by the moon, and always by the salty waters of the sea. I have been mothered by the living, and I have been mothered by the dead, for every soul on the other side, whatever incarnations they have known, whatever bodies they have been, is a mother. To be dead is to remember that we are all each other's mothers.

Raised without any religious indoctrination, I nevertheless was aware growing up of the standard-issue theology about heaven and hell. Yet, even as a child, it made no sense to me. How could someone who was supposedly "good" enjoy the perks of paradise while beneath them other souls broiled in the hellfire of damnation? If you were good, wouldn't you descend into the blazing depths with cool water, a soothing song, a tender hand? Who were those assholes in heaven, I wondered, singing in the clouds self-righteous and smug? To be a mother is to hear the cries of the world and run to our children wherever they are, whoever they are, without exception. To be a mother is to know that no one gets left out of love. We will, in one lifetime or another, make mistakes, commit sins against each other, screw up for sure, and yet our mothers will never stop loving us, never forget who we are and who we might be if only we felt the reality of their love.

My mother, when she appears in my dreams, as she did a few nights ago, is usually about sixty years old. No longer young but not yet in her demented decrepitude. I knew my mother as many bodies—the glamorous dark-haired woman in her forties who nursed me when few mothers did, the sultry seductress putting on makeup at her vanity, the hunched-over old lady navigating the crosswalk with her cane, her hair white, unable to feel her feet, uncertain anymore where she was in time.

I often pray to my mother for help—and I almost always experience her showing up. There's unexpected money for the medical bill, a creative solution to a perplexing problem, a feeling of ease and joy at the holiday gathering. I feel her presence within these everyday miracles, but that doesn't mean I don't still miss her embodied presence. The smell of her that was dirt under her fingernails, roll-on deodorant, the herbs she cut and cooked with, the cat piss that permeated her home, and some intangible something that clung to her coat which for years I kept in my closet so I could bury my face in it and smell her and remember her, until it finally lost all her scent and was just another musty piece of clothing and she was, finally, really gone.

A few nights ago I was feeling overwhelmed with anxieties about the world. I didn't ask for anything in particular, just let out an inchoate cry of "Mummy!" In my dream that followed, I opened a door and there she stood on the threshold, not a vision or some translucent hologram, but her whole physical self. I could smell her, sense what I call the entire umwelt of her soul—her presence, her being, her.

"Can I touch you?" I asked.

She nodded yes.

I had a sense in the dream that for her to appear this fully to me took all her effort and not much was left for speech. She had sent me her body, knowing that it alone could offer the consolations I needed at this moment. I touched her—her softness, her smell, her everything, the very electricity of her being. And she took me in her arms and held me, leading me across the threshold to her world where she cradled me, stroking my hair, and letting me know that all would be well.

"You'll take care of the kids for me, right?" I said in the dream.

She nodded, pulling me close.

"You'll make sure the world is okay?" I begged.

She laughed and without speaking let me know the world would always be safe in her arms.

"I hope you know how much I love you." I lay my head against her breast and exhaled.

My mother stroked my hair, and inside my dream she and I dreamed together of the ten thousand lives we had shared, the ten thousand different ways our souls had reunited in all kinds of bodies. In the past? In the future? Time no longer mattered in her arms. I felt her rough tongue washing my fur, her soft mouth picking me up by the scruff of my neck and carrying me where I needed to go. I felt the huge expanse of her smooth body lifting me through the blue-green depths of the ocean toward the light of the sun. I hid in her pouch while she scrambled across the forest, jounced and bounced, safe against her possum skin. She was the mountain and I was the bear crawling deep inside her to escape the cold. She was the dirt feeding my roots winding through the darkness. She was above me and beneath me, around me and within me. All of our mothers are always that close to our bodies.

Bodies are real. Hearts are real. Mothers are real.

That is the reality my mother and I are talking about now.

# A Message from the Mothers of Magic

Envision yourself as a child playing near the fire as night descends. Mothers circle you, reach out for you when you get too close to the flames, laugh at your pratfalls, take you into their arms when you begin to yawn. These mothers are young and old, male and female, human and other than human. They are the people who cherish you, who recognize your soul, who can tell you who you already are. They know you have arrived at this moment, at this incarnation, at this circle of fire in the darkness as the answer to your prayers—and as the answer to theirs. They can mother because they, too, are circled by mothers.

On the edge of the firelight with the vast darkness of the night behind them is the circle of grandmothers. They are the memory keepers who know that we are held in darkness, move through darkness, return to darkness. They see the flames reflected in your eyes and know that the spark of life always returns. They know you have been a stone, a great tree that fell after the storm, the toad that sat on the moss, still and wise all summer long. Or maybe they know you have been the hummingbird, the dragonfly, and the moth always fluttering, always in motion, always knowing the way forward. They know you are the whale whose songs they heard once at the shore, the nightingale piercing the night with arias, the cricket whose stridulations announce the coming of fall. They know you are their elders returned and you have treasures of wisdom within you that they can help you claim.

These circles of mothers and grandmothers are not there to condition you into conformity and compliance but coax from within you the talents and wonders the community most needs at this moment. This is why you have been reborn. They know that you have arrived in this life with prayers in your heart you have been tending for lifetimes, age after age, incarnation after incarnation. What is it you are here to share?

At the end of the night, when the fire has burned low, they will wrap an ember in damp moss to be carried to the next encampment. Above them, just before dawn, a shooting star traces an arc of light across the blackness.

None among the living know our soul appointments. We do not know when we will leave one life to arrive on time for another. The miscarriages. The accidents. The diseases. The sudden departures that break our hearts. Even when our death is expected, it can still come as a surprise. The living leave the room for a moment, or look out the window, and in an instant a life is done, gone, never to come back. But what if we could see, as the dead do, the journey of the soul from one lifetime to another?

A child dies and another woman in a far-off land conceives. A man is murdered, and soon after his wife discovers she is pregnant—husband and son, one soul, so many lives, and so many different ways to love. A mother succumbs to illness, and years later her grown daughter meets a young woman, perhaps a student in her class or a patient at a hospital or a stranger on the street, and recognizes her, offering back to this soul who was once her mother the mothering she had once received herself.

All our mothers throughout eternity will be circling us when we die, holding our souls as our breath leaves one body and prepares for another. No one dies alone. Whether our lifetime is as inconsequential as a seed planted in the ground that never sprouts or as magnificent as an oak that has seen generations of its seedlings rise tall and mighty as a forest, our souls themselves are unimaginably long. Some lives are small and some are vast, but every soul is long. Every soul matters.

Where are we headed next? What life will we find ourselves inside when we are reborn? Who will be our mother in our next life? The answers to these questions are shrouded in mystery and hidden in our dreams. We know nothing for certain.

Is that little girl drinking water contaminated with lead our next mother? She might be. Is that child hiding during a bombing, filled with terror, haunted by nightmares, one who might give birth to us? Possibly. Could we be reborn into the body of an animal confined to a cage, shackled, force-fed, dying in its own filth even as it labors to give us life? We could.

Bear witness to the world. Do not turn away from the violence, the pollution, the dread, and the horrors. This is the very world into which we will all be reborn. Imagining a way of life outside of the structures and confines of civilization will not be easy. It will take magic; it will take a miracle; it will take each of us becoming the mothers we are called to be. We must hear the cries of our children and answer them.

The world beyond civilization begins the moment we remember that we have been circled by mothers and grandmothers throughout eternity and that we, too, each of us, are mothers. We are all held in the embrace of this *matrisphere*—this round realm for rest and renewal, this soft place to dream and embrace, this cosmic womb where the soul of every being is worthy of care and love and every prayer is always answered. We can step into the mysteries and become the mothers of our grandmothers. We can be reborn into a world of love.

Come into the darkness with us. Kindle the fire with us. Let us recognize the sparks in each other's eyes. Above us the stars burn bright. Beneath us the dirt holds the memories of who we've been.

Within each of us is the mother the world most needs.

Let us together become mothers of the world.

# An Invitation: The Return of Our Mothers

Within the fertile darkness in each of us are seeds waiting for a shift in the temperature, a change in the light, for our soul itself to begin cracking open so they can sprout, grow, and flower. We water such seeds with our attention, our curiosity, our imagination, and our intuition.

## *Recovering the Magic*

- Everyone has things in their lives that feel impossible—forsaken dreams, intractable perplexities, knots that are much too tight. We also have everyday problems and worries that may be small but can still be overwhelming. Begin to acknowledge all of these. Begin the day journaling or fretting out loud about the things that trouble you: about your body, your family, your friends, your work, your home, your car, your neighborhood, your world. Nothing is too small to mention—a phone call, an old ache, a misunderstanding. Nothing is too big either—the state of the justice system, this or that war or genocide, climate change. Just noting these concerns each day, putting them somewhere explicitly either in writing or out loud into the world, is like turning on the faucet within us and helping the water to run clear. We will find we have more and more items on our list, but we will also, miraculously, find things disappearing from it.

- We can bring each of these issues to our mothers and ask for their help. We can admit that we have no control over these things, no ideas for how these problems could possibly be resolved, and no hope for a miracle. But our hopelessness is our mothers' opportunity to show us the magic. Give each problem or issue to someone on the other side—a grandmother, an old aunt, an ancestor of one kind or another. You might want to make a note of who is handling what so that when your prayers are answered you can say thank you to the appropriate soul.

- We might write down our petitions and entrust them to the earth, the fire, the sea, or the wind. We might speak our prayers out loud to a friend. When we do so, we are surrendering to the mysteries of real miracles. We do not know how our prayers will be answered or when our miracle will arrive, only that we can put our faith in the creativity and perspective of all those who love us here and on the other side.

- The more answers we receive, the more our faith will grow. Ultimately, we entrust our souls to our mothers. What is the prayer each of us would carry from one lifetime to another? What treasures from this life do we want our mothers to help us hold on to and claim in our next incarnation? What would we pray for today if we truly knew we had all the time in the world to receive the answer? These questions can transform our lives. We will not answer them quickly, but in the very asking of them we may find ourselves approaching old age and death in a very different spirit.

Miracles give birth to more miracles. A flower grows, blooms, and dies. Its body becomes food for more flowers. Its seeds become a garden over time.

## *Cultivating the Magic*

- Our mothers are waiting to initiate us back into a world where anything can become anything. But they also want us to tap into our own creativity. Each of us will find it in a different medium. We can sing, warble, croon, and enjoy the sound of our own songs. We can smear paint on paper and begin to discover the shapes of the divine. We can tend bees or plant trees. We can dance our way through the world. What do you love making? What have you always wanted to make? It's important to let go of any need for perfectionism or performance. It may take some time experimenting with arts and crafts, taking different classes or workshops, but each of us is creative. In embracing this, we can align ourselves with the creative power of the natural world. Our mothers will help us make things—write, weave, cook, garden, cultivate, sculpt, and imagine. We discover what our ancestral mothers can do the more we ask them to show us what we can do.

- Our mothers know that conception is joyous but labor is often hard. They will guide us through the often long gestation of a project or an idea. Bring together a team to assist with each small step you are taking creatively. On this team may be long-gone friends, former teachers, loving pets. Who can help you bring your creative venture to fruition? Make an altar for this project. Offer your creative endeavors to your mothers on the other side. In turn, they will help us give birth to our dreams.

- When we feel circled by the love and guidance of the old ones, we will find that we have much to offer to others. We will feel less critical and judgmental and more supportive and generous. When we are blossoming as we are meant to, we do not resent others who are in flower.

## *Becoming the Magic*

- Write a letter to your mother in your next incarnation. Tell her who you are and tell her what you have always wanted. What does this mother need to know so that you will be able to fully blossom in your future lives?

- Pour out your heart to this mother, knowing that each day you may be encountering her in the land of the living. Perhaps she is the child next door. Perhaps she is the woman you hear about in the news. Perhaps she is already a girl in your family. Know that every soul you meet might be your mother in your next life.

- What are *your* prayers for your mother already? Do you pray that the water she drinks is uncontaminated? Do you pray that her air is clean? Do you pray she is not scrounging for food in the garbage? Look at the world and know your mother might be at any border, in any bombed-out city—your mother might be anyone. Your prayers for your mother are your prayers for this world. Entrust these prayers to all of your ancestral grandmothers. Know that they are the midwives of magic and miracles. Know that even if we do not know how the world can heal, they can make it happen.

- You may want to create a ritual where you give your letter to the earth, burying it in a place that is special to you on a day that feels particularly sacred. You might travel to a shrine and leave it there or offer it to your mother from this life at her grave or bring it to the land where you hope to be reborn.

- Perhaps you will leave this letter to be read at your own funeral. Perhaps your own mother will hear those words as she sees your body lowered into the ground. Perhaps this letter will be passed down, generation upon generation, so that the woman who will be your mother knows how to recognize you when you return.

- Know that this letter is also a letter to yourself. Know that even now another soul is writing a letter to you, praying to you as a mother. Claim your worthiness, your right to joy, the seeds of desire planted in your heart long ago. Your own mothers are ready to help you do this. Blessings will flow through you in the ten directions. Blessings will flow through you to this soul even now. We have all been each other's mothers, and we will all be each other's mothers in the world to come.

# DEAR MOTHERS TO COME

*Dear Mama,*

*I long to sit on your lap and have you stroke my hair and rub my back. Teach me to be able to speak my mind, to know what I am feeling, and to be able share my emotions with ease and clarity. Dance in the kitchen with me, help me to play and be silly and imagine. I want to walk in the woods with you, to have you teach me the wisdom of plants and flowers. May you already be rooted in the land. May we recognize each other and know the lifetimes we have spent with each other. May we grow roses and magnolias and sunflowers in our garden together, basking in their beauty.*

**—MARY**

*My dear Mother,*

*It feels like it will be an eternity before we meet again, and yet I know it will feel like we were just together when my gaze meets yours. Since you left, the rain has become my mother, the hollowness of grief and the sweetness of memories are what I have left of you. I pray that we recognize each other this next time. How I long to be held in your arms and soothed by your song. I pray that you are free from pain. I pray above all that you are loved by your mother, wherever you are. May we do better next time and each time we are reunited.*

**—NINA**

*My Dearest Future Mother,*

*How many lifetimes have we wandered apart, longing for each other? Who knows how many centuries have passed since that sacred moment when we promised to meet again? Until our paths cross, may all that unsettles your soul or dims your light stay far from you. But I must warn you—I will unsettle you, and I will reshape the rhythm of your days. I hear the rustling of the trees and the song of the waves. They whisper lullabies to your wild spirit. I hope that when*

*I arrive, you will pass these lullabies down to me—the ones you learned from leaves and tides—and that together we will remember how to be wild together.*

**—SENEM**

*Oh Ma,*

*You will have to be brave, and more than brave, to call me in. I can only arrive when you almost stop daring to call for me, to dream for me, to hope for me. You will already have had hopes denied, once, twice, maybe three times. Let me be the one who enters your womb and stays, when the ones who came before me could not. I want a mother courageous and heartbroken. A mother who threw her heart into the wild fire of desire and risked being crushed by grief for the sake of becoming a mother. I want a mother who can show me how grief shapes beauty. As I grow, you will look at me and never see only me—but all that might have been and still might be. Please keep calling for me. It's a heart just like yours that I want to mother mine.*

**—KATHY**

*Beloved Mother,*

*You pour tea for us. The scent of peppermint and thyme, the sweetness of maple and honey and cinnamon. There is so much I want to share, but the purpose of this letter is simply to say I'm here and I know you are here too. We have been preparing ourselves, and all of our children, for this reunion for so many incarnations. I am already here; you have always been here. I will cherish your touch when you hold me again in your arms and cradle me in your lap. When I look into your eyes, you will know what is in my heart. "I have come back home to you."*

**—NICOLE**

*Dearest Mummy,*

*Will we be trees in our next life? Will you protect me with your graceful branches? Will you teach me how to spread my roots and dance with the mycelium? Perhaps we will be whales and you will teach me ocean songs. If we are winds, will you teach me how to be a gentle breeze? Will you show me how to sing with the mountains? And if we are stars, will you glimmer so I always know my way back to you? I pray that you will always remind me that I shine bright and the night sky wouldn't be complete without me.*

**—AGNES**

*Buckle Up, Mom*

*Let's get one thing straight—I will never be yours. Not in the way that means ownership, not in the way that keeps me small, and not in the way that stops me from chasing whatever wild, impossible dream calls my name. I am my own storm. I will always dance. In the kitchen, in the rain, in situations where dancing is wildly inappropriate. I will jump—not because I know where I'll land, but because standing still has never been my thing. Buckle up, Mom. This ride will be fast and messy and loud. You cannot contain me, but you can love me—fiercely, unconditionally, without hesitation. And if you do? If you love me as I am, without trying to smooth my edges or quiet my fire—then I will love you back. With my fierce, all-consuming love. The kind that burns bright, that shakes the earth, that fills every room it enters. Not because I have to, but because I choose to.*

**—JULIE**

*Dear many many mothers,*

*Help me to be born back within the circle of all of you. May each of you see me and know me and help me remember who I already am. Know that even though I return only through one of your bodies, I belong to the body of all of you and I will need, this next time, a circle of mothers to hold me close—to nurse me, to console me, to answer my cries, to laugh with me, to give me the old stories and the old ways. Guide me back to my gifts, help me answer the prayers I have held in my heart for lifetimes, and let us together remember who we really are.*

**—PAM**

*Dearest,*

*I am holding you in my arms. Right now you are so small, just born, and yet you are looking up at my old, wrinkled face and smiling at me with your old dark eyes. We recognize each other, don't we, little one? I kiss your cheek, press your heart close to my heart, and know that soon I will pass, and you will grow, and one day I will come back to another body within your body. Today I give to you the love you will return to me when I return to you. Sleep now, little one, dream, and remember all that we have known together and all that there is left for us to do.*

**—ANNA**

## A HEART SPELL

*Old ones, sea-foam at the shore*

*Old ones, deep forest moss*

*Old ones, old stones*

*Roots woven close together*

*Flocks descending on the lake*

*Wolves howling at night under the stars*

*Stars telling slow stories in the sky*

*Old ones, guide our feet, touch our hearts*

*Help us remember the length of our souls*

*Kindle our kin close*

*Blood kin, soul kin, fur kin, odd kin*

*Kindle our kin in clan and constellation*

*Kindle us close*

*Kindle us close*

*Kindle our kin close*

# ACKNOWLEDGMENTS

To write this book as quickly as I needed to, in nine months, I walked a mountain each day. There are two mountains behind my house—Mt. Overlook and Mt. Guardian. I think of them as two old women who've got the dirt on this part of the world. They know the stories of the stones and remember the ice, the vanished flocks, the forgotten forests, the peoples who knew how to live lightly on the Earth, all of it. Mother Guardian is smaller than Mother Overlook, the path up her body steeper and harder to follow. Because of that, I ran into almost no human beings when I hiked. Each hike I asked for guidance. Each day after having visited with her kin—the oak and hemlock trees, the mountain laurel, the bears and the owls, the salamanders and the ancient fossils in the rocks—I would know what to write. This is their book as much as mine, their prayer as much as mine: our old mountain spell for a world renewed.

So many old mothers arrived to help with all of this. At night in my dreams the seals took me out into the ocean, swimming along mythic coastlines under the stars. Old trees from my childhood, the ones I'd climbed on and read under, guided me underground to the hollows between their roots to show me hidden treasures. A brown house wren sat outside my window as I worked and would circle my head when I stepped outside, no matter the time of day.

I created an altar with photos of mountains and seals and trees and birds and began adding to it as more helpers arrived. The beautiful old woman, Clara Claiborne Park, who taught me Shakespeare in college and invited me over to her house for sherry to talk about poetry, gazed on me with affection and confidence. The letter she sent me after I graduated, encouraging me to continue writing, was a gift that held me through so many literary misadventures. I hope this book embodies the practical guidance she offered a young student on language and voice. Sara Suleri was the extraordinary Pakistani professor that taught me how to think outside of the box and color outside of the lines. I still cannot believe she left so soon, but I will never forget the intellectual mothering she offered to me that I had always wanted. She didn't believe in anything so mundane as a "self," but I hope now she has experienced the wonder of her own remarkable soul. Finally, Cesar Albini, a gay man from Uruguay, was perhaps the most tender and compassionate of mothers I have ever known. That our deepest conversations together took place in front of one of the oldest Black Madonnas in France was lost on me at the time but now makes perfect sense. He was a talented teacher who knew how to call forth from his students abilities they did not know they possessed. Barely a day goes by that I do not miss him and seek to embody his generosity of spirit.

I know his heart would have broken to hear about the young women we lost to despair and addiction in our community while I worked on this book. Their photos are also on my altar and I ask for their help—Jolie, Vanessa, and Rebecca—in creating circles of protection around our daughters and sisters yet to come. Let us help the living to know that no one is ever alone, abandoned, or unloved. May these three graces never be forgotten and always summoned when we feel hopeless and forsaken.

So many of the dead began to show up unexpectedly while I wrote. Most powerful of all was my dear old friend Meg's dear old friend Birdie. Meg shared with me Birdie's journey as cancer ravaged her body. The photo of her, smiling at the end, in her hands a rosary of lapis lazuli and her blue eyes telling the whole world how much love was in her heart, transforms me every time I look at it—even though I never met her in person. I often wondered if it was Birdie who sent my little wren to sing with me.

Just after I sold the proposal for this book, I had a dream of a friend of my mother's, Jane Brooks, leading me into a world of wonders. From a green kitchen, cluttered as hers was in life with books and articles and notebooks filled with poems she'd written, she led me into a vast room of the richest blues and reds from which spun gold mobiles of planets and galaxies and stars. The next day, still filled with the joy of this dream, I walked into a local shop—and there was the exact gold mobile of planets and stars I had seen in that room. I could hear Jane herself, her throaty full-bellied laugh, letting me know that she would always be cheering me on from the other side.

Needless to say, my relationships with my own grandmothers, Nellie and Molly, deepened and widened as I thought and wrote about them. Each morning begins with prayers to them of both petition and gratitude for they are each bountiful with their blessings. My own mother, Patricia Valerie Havens Finn, Gammy Pat to her beloved grandchildren, gave to me an intimate testament to the long story of our souls as I finished writing this book for her. No one is ever lost to us; we all return to each other; we are all each other's mothers returned. May this book in some small way be an expression of gratitude to my mother.

Among the living I have had many fairy godmothers, chief among them my remarkable agent, Leslie Meredith. Leslie is a visionary editor and a canny agent, but she is also a gardener who knows what to weed, when to water, and how to coax authors into bloom. Her attention and care were essential in the writing of this book. That she guided me to the perfect editor was no small feat, and I am blessed in yet another gardener—a rose gardener no less—in my Running Press publisher Shannon Fabricant. I have to admit to being a little surprised when she actually bought this wild as-yet unwritten book. Knowing that her wise eyes would be the first to read it kept me demanding more and more of myself as I wrote. Kate Anderson joined the team as I finished—trimming, questioning, and clarifying until I felt like I was really saying what I'd meant to say all along. I am so grateful for her expert editing.

Thanks as well to the entire Running Press team: Amber Morris for guiding the manuscript through production and Ashley Benning for her careful copy editing. Gratitude as well to my marketing and publicity team including Betsy Hulsebosch, Kara Thornton, and Ana-Maria Bonner. And special thanks to Annie Brag. She is a master connector, helping me with podcasts and events, and I'm grateful for her tireless assistance. Thanks to my visionary cover artist Sarah Jarret whose every piece feels like she is channeling the ancient ones and designer Susan Van Horn for bringing together title and image.

Many years ago I dreamed of a nonhierarchical community that would put children at its center and summon the wisdom of the old mothers. That dream became a prayer, became a book I wrote with my husband, *The Way of the Rose*, became a fellowship of friends from around the world all devoted to the Earth, the rosary, and mothers "by any name you want to call them." My rosebuds, as we call each other, are the living souls with whom I am most intimate. We share our hearts and our heartbreaks, pray for each other through joys and sorrows of all kinds, and together have experienced so many real miracles. "How do you know the Lady is real?" people will sometimes ask me. My truest answer is that I meet her at every Way of the Rose circle I attend. What would I do without my rosebuds? I do not know. But with them, I can do *anything*.

My fellow rosebud Mary Porter Kerns has been with me almost daily on my journey with this book. She's taken all my workshops, built and maintained my website, written her own remarkable book from the perspective of the flowers, read everything I've written, brainstormed with me when I was stuck, and shared the ever-fretting, ever-praying business of being a mother in this crazy world with both laughter and wisdom.

In my life I have often received invaluable mothering from my dearest friends and been awed by their devotion to both their blood and soul kin. Beckie Kravetz showed me how many different ways there are to show up as a mother in the world. Karin Miller-Lewis helped me trust my desire to keep my family close. And HeatherAsh Amara indulged my long meanderings about the long story and radical sobriety while we hiked through clouds of mountain laurel. The artist Dee Mulrooney envisioned for me a devotional image of the old mothers that guided me each day with my writing, reminding me of their power, their beauty, and their wisdom.

I am grateful, too, for the community of readers offered to me on various social media platforms. It's become reflexive to critique these venues for many valid reasons—but there is also so much value as an author in being able to find your audience and engage with them directly. The questions I have been asked, the feedback I've received, and, yes, the praise I've been offered about things I have written have given me the confidence to trust my voice and hone my message. Most of all, my paid Substack subscribers have been there with me through the whole journey of this book, and no writing group I've ever been in was ever better than this attentive and thoughtful cohort.

A special shout-out to Jackie Kellachan and James Conrad who run The Golden Notebook in Woodstock—offering book clubs, author events, and a rich array of titles for voracious readers. Thanks, too, to Audrey Cusson and Jeff Cuiule, purveyors of Mirabai, our local spiritual bookstore and soul sanctuary. These days I find the most interesting book recommendations come from readers, and most of all the readers who are book buyers. I love nothing more than browsing in a bookstore and talking to the managers about what they recommend.

In the midst of all of this reading and writing, Laura Weiss, my yoga teacher, has kept me in my body, has led my body to do things it did not know it could, and helped me recover the memory of other bodies my soul has known. Laura is a genius, a friend beyond measure, and always golden sunshine in my life. Thanks, too, to Corinne Gervai and all the teachers at Euphoria Yoga and Woodstock Infusions for their guidance and care throughout this process.

The many people around the world who have shown up for my classes on working with the ancestral mothers have been essential in the conception of this material, and I am grateful to be able to include so many of their stories in this book. Many thanks, too, to the Shift Network, the Omega Center, and Kripalu, which have supported and promoted my workshops. A shout-out as well to Zoom, which has made connecting with people all over the world possible—although there is nothing like the simple power of touch, of one hand laid over another, at the end of the day.

Which brings me to my husband, Clark Strand, my soulmate through the ages, my writing buddy, my best friend, my lover, my massage therapist, the bringer of coffee to me in bed as the birds begin to sing, crepe-maker extraordinaire, the person I start talking to first thing in the morning and to whom I'm still talking nonstop at the end of the day. We argue, we question, we exchange articles and books and viewpoints, we laugh, we agree, we disagree, we play cards, we fret, we worry, we go for a walk, we worry some more, and always, finally, we hold hands, wrap arms around each other, heart to heart, and pray. "I was raised by a lot of women who adored me," he told me, startlingly, in the middle of Broadway in New York City, on our first date. "Okay then," I answered, utterly stunned by his self-awareness. "Tell me about these women." I had decided already, before I met Clark, that the only answer to the hellscape of civilization was to show up as a mother in the world—but with Clark at my side, our ancestors gathered close, we have discovered together what that vow really means. There will never be enough time for love, but always there will be more time.

Finally, I am grateful to Sophie and Jonah Strand for their endless forgiveness and understanding as I muddled my way through their childhoods, wanting so much for them, demanding too much of myself, making so many mistakes, and so often flailing with frustration. Both of my children, I am proud to say, show up as mothers in the world. My fierce wild girl, Sophie, brings forth from her many challenges spiritual healing for us all through her urgent storytelling, not to mention being my greatest writing friend. My gentle and generous son, Jonah, would feed the world if he could, setting a table where all are welcomed and loved. If anyone can show men how to be mothers, it is this remarkable young man. To these two souls I have been pledged since before this cosmos began; may my prayers for their joy and happiness never end. Wherever they are, they can always call on me. I wrote this book so they would know the truth of that promise.

## NOTES

**[vii] . . . there were nine muses in Greece, nine Icelandic goddesses . . . :** The Muses were not just goddesses of the arts but literally the mothers of invention, creativity, and learning. *Muse* itself is a word that traces back to the root word *men*, "the moon," and as is discussed later in chapter 2, connects these mothers to the imaginative initiation of menstruation.

The nine Icelandic goddesses are also known as the Nine Mothers of Heimdallr, collectively giving birth to a singular deity. The Ennead of the Egyptians consists of both generative male and female gods and includes various figures depending on the particular region and time period. What seems to have been most sacred was the number nine itself.

The nine forms of the goddess Durga are celebrated during a nine-day Hindu festival known as Navratri. A nine-day period of devotion is similarly found in Catholic tradition where a novena, a nine-day prayer period, is offered to a particular saint or expression of the Blessed Mother.

The entire cosmology of the indigenous Kogi people of Colombia is centered on the number nine: nine worlds, nine mothers, nine years of training for the priests that will be known as the Mamas once completed.

What's most striking is not how often the number nine appears in devotion to the ancestral mothers but how rarely scholarship remarks upon its connection to human gestation and its ubiquitous presence behind most religious traditions.

**[7] But when human beings began cultivating crops and hoarding grains . . . :** Many books over the past decades have explored the relationship between agriculture, civilization, and the rise of human violence. Most notable among these is James C. Scott's *Against the Grain* (Yale University Press, 2018).

About ten thousand years or so ago, people began practicing horticulture, deliberately encouraging and spreading certain desirable grains—wheat, barley, rice, and corn. They would return seasonally to the places where these foods grew, as they had always done. At a certain point, however, they became sedentary, growing more and more grain to meet an almost insatiable demand. Because they were no longer migratory and were now depending on a single primary food source, they needed more grain than ever. Such quantities demanded an entirely new kind of large-scale farming and a compliant workforce to tend those fields. If the hunter-gatherer "worked" a few hours each day hunting and gathering, the agriculturalist was sowing, weeding, and harvesting from dawn to dusk. For some time, as Scott documents, most people wanted nothing to do with this backbreaking work and fled back into their accustomed hunter-gatherer lifestyles.

Slavery arose, along with religious threats and enticements as well as other enforcements, to compel most of the populace to labor for the top tier of the community. As soils became predictably depleted, new lands needed to be conquered, colonized, enslaved, and exploited. War and slavery are the foundation of civilization.

**[24] . . . the art critic Sister Wendy declared, "Art never gets better than this.":** Following the art historian and Carmelite nun Sister Wendy Beckett into the paleolithic caves in her documentary *The Story of Painting* is a revelation as she guides viewers to look at the beautifully rendered animals.

My own direct experience of this came through a day spent in the Dordogne with premier archaeologist Christine Desdemains-Hugon, herself an artist turned investigative scientist after her life-changing encounter with paleolithic art. Her book *Stepping-Stones* (Yale University Press, 2010) is a journey into those lost worlds. On a trip in 2015 she took my husband and me into a private cave with no external light and with the palm of her hand turned her flashlight into a flickering candle. A whole world etched into stone came to life around us with animals running and moving and dancing. While many male commentators on paleolithic art will talk about scenes of predator and prey (see Werner Herzog's misguided documentary *Cave of Forgotten Dreams*), the paintings more often depict generative life—the courtship of deer, a pregnant mare, a young mastodon circled by a herd. Desdemains-Hugon posits that these images, repeated over tens of thousands of years, were in themselves sacred and devotional. These people weren't painting what they hunted but what they loved.

The oldest painting, of a warthog in Indonesia, is 51,000 years old. The oldest known musical instrument is a flute found in Spain that may be 67,000 years old. The oldest known story, of the Seven Sisters, otherwise known as the Pleiades, is at least 100,000 years old, which was the last time the seventh star was visible to the naked eye. This story was carried by our migratory ancestors all over the world. The oldest known carved beads are over 150,000 years old. Human civilization is less than 10,000 years old.

**[24] As Barbara Ehrenreich details in her remarkable book *Dancing in the Streets* . . . :** The parallels Ehrenreich draws between the suppression of dancing and revelry and the rise of capitalism and melancholia in *Dancing in the Streets* (Holt, 2007) are astounding. Her book is a call to "collective joy" and the revolutionary power of ecstatic celebration to transform the world.

**[29] A long time ago, when our blood came, we would take ourselves into the caves . . . :** *Blood, Bread, and Roses: How Menstruation Created the World* (Beacon, 1993) by Judy Grahn looks at how paleolithic women, in separating themselves from the community during menstruation so that their blood would not attract predators, began creating both art and math. Grahn posits that the first artistic medium was blood, the first counting was of the moon cycle to prepare for sequestration, and that this connection between the changing body of the woman and the changing body of the moon gave rise to metaphorical thinking.

While much research has been done on the medical uses of placental cord blood, surprisingly little investigation has been done on the healing power of menstrual blood, which is considered taboo by so many patriarchal religious institutions around the world.

**[34] . . . Sheila Na Gig goddesses from Ireland . . . :** A Sheila Na Gig is a figurative carving of a naked woman who is reaching down to part the lips of her vulva and display it. The origins of these carvings are most likely pre-Christian, but they can still be found all across Europe, particularly in Ireland, sculpted into the gates of churches and castles. With audacious facial expressions and a complete lack of self-consciousness, these figures may be traced back to the old crone goddesses whose names have long been lost.

**[36] . . . writes journalist Lucy Cooke in her glorious book *Bitch: On the Female of the Species.*:** *Bitch: On the Female of the Species* (Basic Books, 2023) deconstructs so many anthropocentric ideas about motherhood and what it is supposed to look like. Author Lucy Cooke shows how many different expressions nature has for the maternal—and how many different genders can show up, in so many surprising ways, to ensure the survival of the species. Rigorously researched, this is an essential book for loosening up our own ideas of what being a mother really means.

**[36] As recounted by researcher Helen Fisher, "Sex is almost a daily pastime . . . :** This research is cited in the thought-provoking book *Sex at Dawn* (HarperCollins, 2010) by Christopher Ryan and Cacilda Jethá. Packed with often overlooked evidence from biology and anthropology, it disrupts the idea of human beings as an inherently violent animal, suggesting that it is our disconnection from both bodily pleasure and communal mothering that has brought so much misery into the world. Despite its groundbreaking thesis, the authors' solutions are, to me, unfortunately naive—imagining an easy polyamory uncorrupted by patriarchal systems of dominance. While such behaviors seem to have enriched our distant ancestors, it may be a long time indeed until we have the kind of kinship with each other and the natural world that allows sex to be that uncomplicated again.

**[57] We all begin our lives within our grandmother's bodies.:** As first shown in the key study by Okhura and Okhura in 1970, a woman's eggs are actually formed while she is still a fetus inside her own mother's womb. The egg that will become the grandchild is therefore technically formed inside the grandmother's body.

**[69] . . . the Triple Goddess: the Maiden, the Mother, and the Crone.:** The Triple Goddess, popularized as an idea by mythologist and poet Robert Graves in his book *The White Goddess,* has been taken up enthusiastically by many modern pagans, witches, and feminists although its ancestral origins are obscure. Still, scholars of early spirituality Karl Kerenyi and Marija Gimbutas argue for an ancient devotion to the Triple Goddess as an expression of devotion to the three aspects of the moon (waxing, full, and waning) in its monthly cycle.

**[74] Jezebel, the whore of Babylon . . . :** Lesley Hazleton's *Jezebel: The Untold Story of the Bible's Harlot Queen* (Doubleday, 2007) offers a biography of a woman whose name has been associated with defiant immorality. Using extensive historical research, she reveals a person of extraordinary courage in the face of religious misogyny and fundamentalism. What Hazleton does with this compelling biography is an invitation to all of us to do as we renarrativize the stories of our mothers and grandmothers throughout history.

**[74] Eve is friends with the snake, who has long been the symbol of rebirth and renewal.:** *The Myth of the Goddess: Evolution of an Image* (Penguin, 1993) by Anne Baring and Jules Cashford is the most comprehensive look at the divine mothers through the ages. The chapter on Eve, "The Mother of All Living," offers a thorough examination of the symbolism in the Edenic story and how a generative myth becomes a repressive doctrine. Similarly invaluable are the chapters on Tiamat, Isis, Cybele, and other ancient mothers of the Mediterranean world.

**[75] I have been called Tiamat . . . :** The Enuma Elish, the Babylonian creation myth composed almost four thousand years ago, describes the ascendancy of the god Marduk after the destruction of his grandmother Tiamat. She is often described as the dark chaos of the ocean depths. When she mingles with the god Apsu, who represents the fresh spring waters coming from the mountains, life itself begins. Eventually her grandson Marduk, drunk on beer, will "split her like a shellfish" by thrusting a spear into her heart.

This story is the basis for the opening of Genesis where God divides the waters of creation. The word *tehom* to describe the "face of the deep" has its derivation in Tiamat's name—although the grandmother herself has disappeared and the primal violence has been abstracted into an organizing necessity.

One of the big questions about early agriculture and the cultivation of grain is whether or not the motivation was the baking of bread or the brewing of beer. The Enuma Elish would seem to posit the latter as our actual original sin. For an in-depth look at the entanglement of intoxication and civilization, see Edward Slingerland's *Drunk: How We Sipped, Danced, and Stumbled Our Way to Civilization* (Hachette, 2021).

**[88] . . . the crime women were most often accused of during the Burning Times . . . :** In her invaluable book *Witchcraze: A New History of the*

*European Witch Hunts* (HarperOne, 1995), scholar Anne Barstow documents how often women were suspect for consulting with their deceased mothers and grandmothers—as their ancestors had done throughout the ages. Barstow's examination of this period of horrific violence against women is both comprehensive and intimate. As often as she can, she names these women, shares what she knows about their lives, and looks at what was done to them in the name of justice and piety. Nevertheless, as she herself bemoans, she is only one of a few scholars who have done the research to recover these stories. We need many more books and much more scholarship about what actually happened during these centuries of violence.

**[90] . . . for witchcraft at Pendle Hill, less than a day's journey from her home.:** In 1612 nine women and a man were executed for being witches in the Pendle Hill area of Lancashire, England. There were many other accusations and murders during this period, but this was one of the more famous trials, given the sheer number of people found guilty and murdered. All of this was happening as King James I issued his definitive version of the Bible and published his book *Daemonologie* in order to root out heretics and demons, mostly women, in his realm. Over five hundred women would be killed as witches during the seventeenth century in England.

**[91] One young mother, Alyse Young, successfully nursed her daughter through the illness.:** Alyse was thirty-two, the mother of a seven-year-old, when she was tried and hung for witchcraft in Hartford, Connecticut, in 1649. There is no extant record of the trial so the specific accusations against her remain a mystery. One theory is that there was a bad flu that year which felled young and old alike, including many in the local preacher's family. Alyse successfully protected and healed her own child. Her husband abandoned her to her fate, and thirty years later her daughter was also accused of witchcraft, although she managed to avoid execution. It's important to note that women may have been accused, and even murdered, as witches earlier than this in the colonies—before the practice of keeping public records.

**[94] "Her mother called her Jehanne," they'd say, "and her father called her D'arc.":** Joan of Arc has mesmerized people since she first emerged from her home of Domrémy to save France. But trying to see Joan fully means pulling aside the veil of piety the Church covered her in when it sainted her in 1920—almost five hundred years after it had decreed that she should be burned at the stake as a heretic and a witch. Joan is the only saint officially beatified by the Church who was also tried, condemned, and executed by the same priestly authority. Much about her remains mysterious.

Most of what we know about Joan comes from the transcripts of her trial and the transcripts of the second trial that her mother, Isabelle Romée, devoted the rest of her life to making happen. At Notre-Dame in Paris, twenty years after she had been killed, Joan was fully exonerated. As much information as we have about Joan from these transcripts, however, it is important to remember what was *not* being said—by Joan herself and by those who loved her. Joan wanted to protect herself; her champions wanted the world to cherish her; and the ecclesiastical court was a very dangerous place for a woman who received, as she described it, "council" from the other side.

The most interesting biographies in English of Joan were written before she was sainted and are able to acknowledge the Church as her real enemy. Mark Twain (*Joan of Arc*) and Bernard Shaw (*St. Joan*) were amazed by the sharpness of her wit and the depth of her wisdom. Vita Sackville-West's biography (*Saint Joan of Arc*) is the most thorough and readable. A strange little book written in the middle of the nineteenth century by an American pastor grapples with the complexities of Joan with real insight. *The Wonderful Story of Joan of Arc and the Meaning of Her Life for All Americans* by C. M. Stevens recognizes Joan, not as a saint, but a divine counterpart to Jesus.

Scholar and mystic Ean Begg in his book *The Cult of the Black Virgin* (Arkana, 1985) taps into the lore swirling around Joan when she was alive. He connects her to the legends of the Cathars and begins to question the very significance of her name, *D'arc*, suggesting that it was Joan herself who was the holy grail. In a conversation with me before he died, Ean Begg elaborated on his thoughts about all of this with me.

[96] **Less than ten years after Jehanne's murder, they began printing the Bible . . . :** Before the invention of the printing press people were still embedded in the oral wisdom of their ancestors—after 1440 they were increasingly indoctrinated into the inherently misogynistic tenets and beliefs of the Bible. Leonard Shlain in his book *The Alphabet Versus the Goddess: The Conflict Between Word and Image* (Penguin, 1998) explicates his thesis that the ways in which the introductions of new forms of media—from the phonetic alphabet to the printing press to industrial book production—initiate eruptions of violence. Shlain, a neuroscientist, explores how each successive invention has shifted our thinking from the right to the left brain, from the concrete and the holistic to the abstract and the compartmentalized. Shlain died in 2009, before the rise of social media, but his work would predict a world subsequently becoming more fearful and more aggressive.

[116] **". . . each Dalai Lama leaves signs . . ." :** Tibetan Buddhism has a tradition of reincarnation. Before a lama, or teacher, passes, he will leave particular signs to various individuals for finding his next embodiment. In the movie about the Dalai Lama *Kundun* by Martin Scorsese, a group of high priests arrive at a small dwelling and begin testing a young boy—asking him to identify "his" rosary or spectacles for instance. This

institutionalized expression of the soul's return was probably once ubiquitous and less about controlling the transfer of power than recognizing the embodiment of our beloveds come back to us.

[117] **Once your people made images of their grandmothers' bodies to hold in their hands.:** Among the oldest human depictions in the world are the so-called "goddess" figurines found throughout Europe and Asia. Made from clay and soft stone, they all depict naked women's bodies. Looking at many of them, however, one is struck by breasts and bellies of all shapes and sizes that have clearly borne children. These are the bodies not of adolescent girls but of mature women, many of them probably grandmothers. Of note, as well, is that almost all of these ancient figurines are of a size that one could hold in the palm of one's hand—for reassurance, consolation, and connection.

[117] **Their Madonnas bared their breasts to nurse their children. They stood with jaunty hips to hold their toddlers steady.:** Prior to the modern age, the Virgin Mary was often depicted as Maria Lactans, the nursing mother. Not only were her breasts often bare, but she would frequently be expressing milk into the mouth of her child—or even the priests and their congregations.

To explore the ways in which the Virgin Mary has been transformed and marginalized in the modern era see *Missing Mary: The Queen of Heaven and Her Re-Emergence in the Modern Church* (Macmillan, 2004) by Charlene Spretnak.

[119] **Look at that popular image of the one you call the Virgin Mary again. Really look at it. Look at how she appears on the Miraculous Medal.:** The Miraculous Medal of the Virgin Mary was transmitted to the French nun Catherine Labouré during a series of apparitions in 1830. This image of a submissive Madonna, her head downcast and her

arms spreading her robes wide, has become one of the most ubiquitous depictions of the Blessed Mother—recreated on pendants, statuary, and paintings. As any number of feminist artists have shown, however, this seemingly submissive woman is an almost perfect rendition of a human vulva with its clitoris and labia.

For a more detailed exploration on the history of this image and the other ancient mysteries hidden within it, please see the chapter "Expect a Miracle" in my book with Clark Strand, *The Way of the Rose: The Radical Path of the Divine Feminine Hidden in the Rosary* (Spiegel & Grau, 2019).

**[124] The dead can see in the ten directions.:** The ten directions is a Buddhist term referring to the eight compass directions (north, south, east, west, northeast, northwest, southeast, southwest) as well as up and down.

**[133] . . . the ice ages, the volcanic eruptions, the falling of the stars.:** Most of human history has gone unrecorded. Our own species is at least 100,000 years old, and of that time we know the events of only a few millennia. Nevertheless, the Earth itself holds a story of cataclysmic changes that our ancestors almost certainly endured and survived. For a marvelous journey through deep time see Thomas Halliday's *Otherlands* (Random House, 2022) which transports readers back through epochs and extinctions to the very beginnings of life on this planet.

**[140] Only of course the whole study was bogus . . . :** The podcast *Maintenance Phase* has the single best episode, "The French Paradox," on debunking this initially lauded and eventually criticized study from the nineties about the health benefits of red wine.

**[143] But the first crop that Columbus planted on Hispaniola was sugarcane.:** If organized agriculture introduced slavery to the world, the labor-intensive demands of sugar production ensured its escalation and necessity. Even today, sugar production often involves an indentured population subjected to horrific violence. *Sweetness and Power: The Place of Sugar in Modern History* (Viking, 1985) by Sidney W. Mintz is an eye-opening look at the cruelties and costs of a spoonful of sweetness.

**[165] One scientist, Mark Blumberg, suspects that we are "learning how to have a body.":** Amanda Gefter's article in *The New Yorker* (August 31, 2023) "What Are Dreams For?" is an in-depth exploration of Blumberg's experiments and theories.

# RAISING READERS

## Books Build Bright Futures

Thank you for reading this book and for being a reader of books in general. As an author, I am so grateful to share being part of a community of readers with you, and I hope you will join me in passing our love of books on to the next generation of readers.

**Did you know that reading for enjoyment is the single biggest predictor of a child's future happiness and success?**

More than family circumstances, parents' educational background, or income, reading impacts a child's future academic performance, emotional well-being, communication skills, economic security, ambition, and happiness.

Studies show that kids reading for enjoyment in the US is in rapid decline:

- In 2012, 53% of 9-year-olds read almost every day. Just 10 years later, in 2022, the number had fallen to 39%.
- In 2012, 27% of 13-year-olds read for fun daily. By 2023, that number was just 14%.

Together, we can commit to **Raising Readers** and change this trend. How?

- Read to children in your life daily.
- Model reading as a fun activity.
- Reduce screen time.
- Start a family, school, or community book club.
- Visit bookstores and libraries regularly.
- Listen to audiobooks.
- Read the book before you see the movie.
- Encourage your child to read aloud to a pet or stuffed animal.
- Give books as gifts.
- Donate books to families and communities in need.

BOB1217

**Books build bright futures**, and **Raising Readers** is our shared responsibility.

For more information, visit **JoinRaisingReaders.com**

Sources: National Endowment for the Arts, National Assessment of Educational Progress, WorldBookDay.org, Nielsen BookData's 2023 "Understanding the Children's Book Consumer"